P9-BYS-578

In
Defense
of Liberty

The Reverend Martin Luther King Jr. greets a crowd of 200,000 peaceful demonstrators at the Civil Rights March on Washington, D.C., where he delivered his famous I Have a Dream speech, August 28, 1963. *AP/Wide World Photos*

In Defense of Liberty

The Story of America's Bill of Rights

RUSSELL FREEDMAN

HOLIDAY HOUSE / New York

Library of Congress Cataloging-in-Publication Data
Freedman, Russell.
In defense of liberty: the story of America's Bill of Rights / Russell Freedman.—1st ed.
p. cm.
Summary: Describes the origins, applications of, and challenges to the ten amendments to the
United States Constitution that comprise the Bill of Rights.
Includes bibliographical references and index.
ISBN 0-8234-1585-6 (hardcover)
1. United States. Constitution. 1st–10th Amendments—History—Juvenile literature.
2. Civil rights—United States—History—Juvenile literature. [1. United States. Constitution.
1st–10th Amendments. 2. Constitutional amendments. 3. Civil rights.] I. Title.

KF4750.F74 2003
342.73'085—dc21
2002191918

To George Weller
In friendship, and for our many
conversations about civil liberties

ACKNOWLEDGMENTS

For advice and instruction concerning legal concepts and terminology, I am grateful to Ellen Levine, Abbe R. Tiger, and Peter V. Rajsingh.

My thanks to the following for help in obtaining photographs and other illustrations: Joan Carroll, AP/Wide World Photos; Jemal Creary, Corbis/Bettmann; Dana Signe K. Munroe, the Rhode Island Historical Society; Allen Reuben, Culver Pictures, Inc.; the Library of Congress, Prints and Photographs Division; the National Archives; the New York Public Library; Stock Montage, Inc.

Special thanks to George Weller for finding helpful research material and obtaining a rare photograph of the nation's last public hanging; to Michael L. Cooper for his energetic help with picture research in Washington; and to my stalwart and tireless editor, Regina Griffin, who suggested the idea for this book and its prequel, *Give Me Liberty!: The Story of the Declaration of Independence*.

CONTENTS

Can schoolchildren be required to salute
the American flag and recite the Pledge of Allegiance?

Can a rap group be prosecuted for using "obscene" lyrics?

Does the Constitution give individuals
the right to keep and bear arms?

Do school officials need a warrant
from a judge to search students?

Do minors accused of a crime have
the same constitutional rights as adults?

Does the Constitution allow school officials to use
physical punishment, such as spanking or paddling,
as a form of discipline?

Does the Constitution allow the execution
of a mentally retarded person?

Does the Bill of Rights guarantee a right to personal privacy?

1. A Knock on the Door in the Middle of the Night

Imagine that you are sound asleep, adrift in the ebb and flow of dreams. But something is disturbing you. Somewhere at the edges of your dreamworld, a distant pounding grows louder and louder.

You awake with a start. Police are pounding on your door, shouting for you to open up! It is four o'clock in the morning.

They burst into the house, push you against the wall, and frisk you. Then you are handcuffed. A black hood is slipped over your head and you are led outside to a waiting car, which carries you off to a secret detention center.

No one knows where you are being held, or why, or how to get any information about you. Confined to a cramped dark cell, you lose all track of time. You can hear the shuffling of feet outside in the corridor and, at times, the muffled cries of prisoners being beaten or tortured.

Finally you are taken to a windowless room where teams of interrogators are waiting to question you. You sit facing a blinding light. So far, you have not been charged with a crime or told why you have been arrested.

Someone somewhere has accused you of something. But who? And what? Was it something you said? A meeting you attended? A book you borrowed? A phone call that the police overheard?

You are not allowed to call a lawyer, to confront your accusers, or to see what evidence, if any, there is against you. You will have to prove your innocence alone, without knowing what the accusations are.

The questioning begins. . . .

A nightmare? Secret arrests on secret evidence, secret trials, and even secret executions have always been ugly facts of life in parts of the world where people have few if any rights.

Can it happen here? Can it happen to you?

America's Bill of Rights—462 words written two centuries ago—was intended to protect ordinary citizens from the abuses of governmental power. Those words promise the basic civil liberties that all Americans enjoy as their birthright and that no government, however powerful, can legally take away.

Most Americans today take it for granted that they can speak their minds freely, worship as they please, criticize those in power, and expect fair treatment under the law. But those rights have not always been respected or enforced. The struggle to fully realize the ideals expressed in the Bill of Rights has been carried on by countless individuals who have had the courage to stand up for their rights, often at great personal risk—from former slaves seeking to breathe real meaning into emancipation to the freedom riders and civil rights advocates of recent times. They have helped establish the living body of law that to this day keeps most of us free.

Without the Bill of Rights, we might wake up in the dead of night to find that we do, in fact, live in a nightmare world.

2. Why We Have the Bill of Rights

"A bill of rights is what the people are entitled to against every government on earth . . . and what no just government should refuse."

—*Thomas Jefferson*

The story of America's Bill of Rights begins in England with an unpopular king named John, who ruled eight centuries ago. In those days, the kings of England—like most of the world's rulers—held almost unlimited powers. The king's word was law. He could do just about anything he wanted to do. He could take away your land and possessions, throw you into a dungeon, and even have you killed—all without giving a reason.

The king's power was very great indeed, but it wasn't absolute. He shared his power with the church and with the landowning barons and other nobles who had sworn their allegiance to the Crown. The ordinary folks of England, who spent their lives toiling from dawn to dusk on the barons' lands, had no say in who held power. And they had no rights or liberties that they could count on.

King John was a tyrant, a mean and selfish man who made plenty of enemies. He extorted money from his subjects to pay for his military adventures overseas, and he plundered baronial estates, taking food, farm animals, wood, and equipment without payment whenever he pleased. By 1215, the barons were fed up with the way John was ruling the realm. They rose in overwhelming force, took London, and forced John to meet them in a meadow called Runnymede on the south bank of the Thames River.

KING IOHN.

There they confronted the king with a long list of grievances. And they demanded that John grant certain rights to them in writing. Otherwise, they would renounce their allegiance to him.

John saw that he had to give in to the barons' demands or be driven from the throne. So he agreed to a list of rules that he would obey in running the kingdom. In June 1215, at Runnymede, John affixed his royal seal to the document that the barons had drawn up. They called it the Magna Carta, Latin for the Great Charter.

Anyone reading the Magna Carta today might wonder why it is recognized as a great milestone on the road to liberty. The document contains no lofty principles or idealistic language. It did little to help the common people of England. It dealt mainly with the complaints of the wealthy barons who

had dared to challenge the king. And yet the Magna Carta has had a lasting influence on the imaginations of succeeding generations, because it introduced the idea of writing human rights into law.

By spelling out certain rights, the charter placed written legal limits on the king's power. Nothing like that had ever happened before. The king was no longer free to do anything he wanted. He was no longer above the law, but had promised to obey those written rules like any other Englishman.

While the barons were the ones who benefited at first, the Magna Carta granted rights that eventually would be claimed by all English citizens. For example, the charter said that the king could not seize property belonging to the barons without fair compensation. And it said that no one could be punished or jailed "except by the lawful judgment of his peers, and by the law of the land."

From then on, a continuing struggle for power took place between England's rulers and the English people, as represented by an elected Parliament. Again and again, the people wrested from their rulers declarations of rights that reinforced the principles first established in the Magna Carta. Gradually the idea grew that the people possessed certain fundamental rights that no king, no government, could violate.

Eventually, the rivalry between Parliament and the Crown led to a bloodless revolution that brought King William and Queen Mary to the throne. The British called it the Glorious Revolution. In 1689, William and Mary agreed to sign an English Bill of Rights that spelled out the basic principles of English freedom and made Parliament more powerful than any occupant of the royal throne. After 1689, no British monarch could legally violate the rights established by the English Bill of Rights.

By that time, the idea of individual rights and liberties guaranteed by written law had crossed the Atlantic and taken root in the New World. Settlers from England were colonizing America in ever-increasing numbers. They considered themselves English citizens entitled to all their rights under English law. Even those settlers who came from Holland, Germany,

Following the Glorious Revolution in England, King William and Queen Mary signed the English Bill of Rights, enacted by Parliament in 1689.
Picture Collection, The New York Public Library

France, and other countries soon grew accustomed to living under English customs and laws, and they too came to believe that English rights were their rights.

During the 1700s, the American settlers began to complain that British authorities were trampling on their rights. Taxes were being imposed on the colonists by a distant Parliament in which they were not represented and had no say. British soldiers and customs inspectors were invading people's homes whenever they pleased, in search of smuggled goods, or contraband. Colonists who criticized the government were being charged with crimes

British policies in the Americas provoked angry colonial opposition. This wood engraving from a book published in 1850 depicts a Stamp Act protest in New York during the 1760s. The skull-and-crossbones banner says, "England's Folly & America's Ruin."
The Library of Congress

and stripped of their right to trial by jury. These grievances and many others fanned the flames of colonial resentment against British rule.

In 1776, mounting opposition to the unchecked power of the British government erupted into revolution. The colonists broke their ties with the mother country and declared their independence. They were ready to fight

England to establish a new government that would guarantee their precious rights and freedoms.

With independence, each of the thirteen colonies became a sovereign state. When an American referred to his "country," he meant his home state, such as Virginia or Massachusetts. During the Revolutionary War, those sovereign states joined together under the Articles of Confederation, the document adopted in 1781 that created the first government of the United States. But when peace came, the Confederation proved too weak to hold the separate states together by anything stronger than, as George Washington said, "a feeble thread." And so the states' leaders agreed to attend a national Constitutional Convention. They hoped to create a strong central government that would unite the thirteen states and meet the new nation's pressing needs.

In May 1787, fifty-five political leaders from every state except Rhode Island (which refused to attend) gathered in Philadelphia, which, with forty thousand people, was the biggest city in North America. George Washington, an imposing figure at six foot two, a hero of the Revolutionary War, and a man of few words, was chosen president of the convention. Washington was fifty-five. Over half the delegates were men under forty. Benjamin Franklin, at eighty-one, was by far the oldest. Suffering from a variety of ailments, he had trouble walking and was carried to the daily meetings through the streets of Philadelphia in a sedan chair balanced on long poles held aloft by prisoners from the local jail.

The delegates met in the Pennsylvania State House, now called Independence Hall, from May 25 to September 17—sixteen sultry weeks of debate, deliberation, and compromise as they discussed how best to govern themselves. Along with the stifling heat and humidity, the State House was invaded at times by giant flies and mosquitoes that could bite right through the delegates' long silk stockings.

At eighty-one, Benjamin Franklin was the oldest delegate to the Constitutional Convention, held in Philadelphia in 1787.
The National Archives

To start with, the delegates agreed to scrap the Articles of Confederation and begin from scratch; they would create an entirely new constitution designed to govern the nation. They worked behind closed doors, holding their meetings in secrecy because they did not want to be pressured by public opinion. In secret discussions, a delegate could change his mind or advocate an unpopular position without fear of embarrassment. "No constitution would ever have been adopted . . . if the debates had been made public," James Madison of Virginia said years later. Madison attended every meeting, sat close to the front, and kept careful notes, so thanks to him, we know a great deal about what went on at the convention.

Because the delegates feared the abuses of unchecked governmental power, they thought deeply and argued endlessly over who should have power and how much. In the past, certain rights had been granted *to* the people by the king or by Parliament, and those rights could as easily be taken away. Distrustful of power in all its forms, the early Americans turned this notion of government on its head. In the United States, all branches of government would receive their authority *from* the people. That is why the preamble to the Constitution—the document's very first words—names "We, the people" as the authors of the Constitution and as the government's ultimate source of power.

The proposed Constitution was to be the supreme law of the land, a set of principles and rules that no government official could violate. Liberty

George Washington, a hero of the Revolutionary War, was elected president of the Constitutional Convention. *The Library of Congress*

Slaves working in a cotton field. The man with the gun at his knees fires to scare off birds that might eat the newly planted seeds. From a wood engraving in *Harper's Weekly*, 1875. *The Library of Congress*

would be protected by dividing the powers of the national government among three separate branches—the Congress, the presidency, and the federal courts. A complex system of checks and balances would prevent any single branch from becoming too powerful.

And yet the Constitution, as it took shape, was not to everyone's liking. One troublesome controversy concerned the presence in America of an enslaved African population. At least twenty-five of the fifty-five delegates to the Constitutional Convention were slave owners.

How could political leaders creating a new government seek liberty for themselves while they denied it to others? Many of the delegates were opposed to slavery as an affront to the ideals of liberty that the Constitution claimed to protect. George Mason of Virginia, himself a slave owner, condemned "the infernal traffic" of enslaved Africans and warned that slavery would bring "the judgment of heaven" down on the nation. And yet condemning slavery was one thing; ending it was quite another.

The delegates from the South, whose plantations and way of life depended on slave labor, threatened to walk out of the convention if the proposed Constitution prohibited slavery. They warned that if slavery were outlawed, Georgia, South Carolina, and North Carolina would "not be parties to the Union." And so the delegates gave in to what they saw as political reality. Convinced that they could not abolish slavery and still form

A 1796 engraving shows
the punishment of a
"mutinous slave."
Picture Collection,
The New York Public Library

a strong union, they agreed to a compromise. The slave trade would be permitted for another twenty years, until 1808, when finally it would be banned. But slavery itself would be tolerated under the Constitution; it would continue until America's Civil War of 1861 to 1865.

Another hotly contested issue was the absence of a bill of rights in the proposed Constitution. Included within the body of the document were several provisions protecting individual rights, but the Constitution said nothing about such basic civil liberties as freedom of speech, religion, or the press. Most of the states already had bills of rights written into their own constitutions, so many delegates felt that a national bill of rights wasn't needed. Even so, this omission made some of the delegates uneasy, since the states were about to hand over many of their powers to the national government.

George Mason, the Virginia slave owner who earlier had condemned slavery, now rose to speak in favor of a national bill of rights. "It would give great quiet to the people," he said, and probably could be written in "a few hours" by using the various state constitutions as models. Mason had himself written a bill of rights for Virginia's constitution. His suggestion was supported by Elbridge Gerry of Massachusetts, but the delegates, weary after four months of debate, voted the idea down.

On September 17, 1787, the delegates were finally ready to vote on the new Constitution. Ben Franklin admitted that the document wasn't perfect. "I confess that there are several parts of this Constitution which I do not at present approve," he said. "But I am not sure I shall never approve them." He urged all the delegates to join him in signing the document to show the nation that they agreed in principle.

Three delegates—George Mason and Edmund Randolph of Virginia, and Elbridge Gerry of Massachusetts—refused to sign. They felt that the new government would be too powerful to respect the rights of the states or the liberties of individuals. Mason claimed that he would rather chop off his right hand than put it to the Constitution as it then stood. But most of the delegates voted to back the document, and copies were sent out to each of the states for their approval. The compact had to be ratified, or approved, by at least nine of the thirteen states before it could become the supreme law of the land.

As the newly drafted Constitution circulated in the states, the demand for a national bill of rights became a popular cause among those early Americans who had lived without a bill of rights and had suffered because of it. At the special state conventions called to ratify the document, and in the nation's newspapers and journals, the people made it clear that they wanted protection against abuses by the central government. From his

George Mason, a Virginia planter and slave owner, demanded an end to the "wicked, cruel, and unnatural" slave trade. Disappointed when his proposal for a bill of rights was voted down, Mason was one of three delegates who refused to sign the proposed Constitution. *The Library of Congress*

Signing the Constitution on September 17, 1787. *The Library of Congress*

diplomatic post in Paris, where he was serving as American ambassador to France, Thomas Jefferson wrote to James Madison: "A bill of rights is what the people are entitled to against every government on earth . . . and what no just government should refuse."

Madison had been one of those who felt that a bill of rights wasn't necessary, but Jefferson's letter helped change his mind. He worried now that the Constitution would be rejected unless it included specific guarantees to protect individual liberties. So he promised to make a bill of rights the first order of business when the new Congress met. Only by making such a promise were the Constitution's supporters able to gain the approval of the necessary number of states.

Fortunately, the Constitution is not a rigid document set in stone. The framers, or authors, wanted it to be flexible enough to allow for changing times and new ideas. So they came up with a way to introduce constitutional amendments, or improvements. And since they didn't want the document to be subject to every passing whim, they made certain that the amendment process required widespread agreement. Amendments must be approved by two-thirds of the members of Congress and must then be ratified by three-fourths of the state legislatures.

Madison kept his promise. When the new nation's first Congress met in New York in 1789, he proposed the constitutional amendments that would become known as the Bill of Rights. Madison was a diminutive man, five foot four, with a pale complexion and a reedy voice. But he made an eloquent speech. He acknowledged the popular demand for a bill of rights. And he agreed that if governmental powers were not limited by a higher law, then individual rights could never be secure.

James Madison, known as the Father of the Bill of Rights. Madison later served two terms as president of the United States, from 1809 to 1817.
The National Archives

The rights proposed by Madison were taken from the Virginia Declaration of Rights, from other states' bills of rights, and from the English Bill of Rights. After committees of the House of Representatives and the Senate made some changes, Congress adopted twelve of Madison's amendments, which were sent to the state legislatures and debated for more than two years.

Two of the amendments were rejected by the states, because they dealt with matters that had nothing to do with people's personal rights—they concerned congressional salaries and how the number of representatives to Congress from each state would be determined. They were dropped from the bill. The remaining ten amendments were ratified by the states, and the Bill of Rights—the first ten amendments to the Constitution—became part of the highest law of the land on December 15, 1791.

For the first time in history, people organizing a government made sure to claim certain rights for themselves as individuals—rights that their government could not alter or take away. And yet the original Bill of Rights fell far short of the noble ideals it proclaimed. While the authors of the Constitution were political revolutionaries, they were also men of their time whose vision of the world was filtered through the customs and beliefs of colonial America. When they declared a government in the name of "We, the people," they weren't really thinking of all the people. In the 1790s, the liberties guaranteed by the Bill of Rights did not apply to everyone. Whole groups of people were left out.

Women, at that time, were shut out of public life. They weren't allowed to vote, hold public office, or even attend town meetings. When Thomas Jefferson announced in the Declaration of Independence that "all men are created equal," few people gave much thought to women's rights. Women were seen as second-class citizens, at best. The Bill of Rights would be in force for nearly 130 years before women in America won the right to vote, in 1920.

Native Americans were not considered citizens of the new nation, and were completely unprotected by the Constitution and the Bill of Rights.

This nineteenth-century drawing shows a colonial New England kitchen,
the domain of women, children, and elderly men.
The Library of Congress

Viewed as an alien people, they would be militarily defeated, stripped of most of their land, and confined to reservations. It wasn't until 1924 that Congress finally granted all American Indians U.S. citizenship.

Enslaved Africans and their descendants had no rights and no protections under the original Bill of Rights. Slaves were regarded as human property, not citizens. And while many political leaders at the time had denounced slavery, the Constitution failed to outlaw the practice. The principles of liberty and equality on which the Constitution was based did not apply to enslaved Africans.

It would take a bloody Civil War, and then a century more of struggle, before African Americans began to enjoy the full freedoms promised by the Bill of Rights.

THE FIRST
AMENDMENT

PART ONE

*Congress shall make no law respecting an establishment
of religion, or prohibiting the free exercise thereof.*

3. Freedom of Religion

"One's right to life, liberty, and property, to free speech, a free press, freedom of worship and assembly, and other fundamental rights may not be submitted to a vote; they depend on the outcome of no elections." — *Supreme Court, 1943*

In 1942, during the early days of World War II, religious liberty in America met one of its toughest tests. Overseas, American troops were battling Japanese forces in the Pacific and would soon attack Adolf Hitler's armies in North Africa. On the home front, schoolchildren stood at their desks every morning and took part in a patriotic ritual: they saluted the American flag and recited the Pledge of Allegiance.

At a school in Charleston, West Virginia, two sisters, Marie and Gatha Barnett, were sent to the principal's office when they refused to salute and recite the Pledge of Allegiance with the other children. As Jehovah's Witnesses, the girls had been taught that saluting the flag would violate the biblical command to worship no "graven images"—images that are not sacred, including flags.

School officials insisted that all students, without exception, must take part in the patriotic exercise, and they were backed up by a local law. Marie and Gatha were expelled. Taunted by their classmates, they were called "traitors," "Nazis," "Japs," and worse.

They weren't the first. Jehovah's Witness children, supported by their parents, had been refusing to salute the flag for years, saying that it was against their deeply held religious beliefs. By 1942, some two thousand young Witnesses had been expelled from schools across the country.

"I do not salute the flag, not because I do not love my country, but . . . I

The claim of Jehovah's Witness schoolchildren that saluting the flag
and reciting the Pledge of Allegiance violated their religious beliefs led to
a landmark Supreme Court case. *Corbis/Bettmann*

love God more, and I must obey His commandments," wrote ten-year-old
William Gobitas. The expelled children thought that as Americans, they
had a right to refuse. But the laws said no, and in 1940, in a case called
Minersville School District v. [for *versus*] *Gobitis* (the name was misspelled in
court records), the United States Supreme Court had upheld those laws.

With the onset of World War II, refusals to salute the flag triggered an
ugly wave of anti-Witness hysteria. In one week alone, the Justice Department received hundreds of reports of physical assaults on Jehovah's Wit-

nesses. Witness children were followed home, jeered at, and at times, beaten by classmates. In Richwood, West Virginia, the police forced nine Witnesses to swallow large amounts of castor oil when they refused to salute the flag. One of the worst incidents took place in Kennebunk, Maine, where a mob of 2,500 people sacked and burned the local Jehovah's Witness church.

But in turn, these violent actions aroused a backlash. The Supreme Court's 1940 decision was widely criticized by legal scholars, by newspaper editors, and even by organizations as staunchly patriotic as the American Legion. And by the time Marie and Gatha Barnett were expelled from school in 1942, three of the Supreme Court justices who had ruled against the Witnesses had indicated that they may have changed their minds.

Hoping to overturn the 1940 ruling, attorneys for the Witnesses selected Marie and Gatha as a test case and won a new hearing before the Court. They claimed that the law requiring Witness children to salute the flag violated their constitutional rights under the First Amendment.

Ten-year-old Billy Gobitas wrote to the school board in Minersville, Pennsylvania, explaining why he felt he could not salute the flag. The Supreme Court ruled against Billy in 1940 but agreed to reconsider in 1942. *The Library of Congress*

The First Amendment guarantees five fundamental freedoms, and of these, the first is freedom of religion. The amendment prohibits Congress from establishing an official religion or interfering with anyone's right to worship freely.

The early Americans understood what it means to be denied religious liberty. Many of them sailed to the New World to escape religious persecution in the Old. State-sponsored churches were the rule throughout Europe, and often, other religions were forbidden. In England during the reign of the Catholic Queen Mary I (1553 to 1558), some three hundred Protestants, old and young, women and men, were burned at the stake. The queen became known as "Bloody Mary."

And yet all too often, settlers in America found that religious intolerance had accompanied them across the ocean. Colonists who had been seeking the freedom to worship as they pleased did not always respect the religious practices of others. Most of the early colonies established official government-sponsored churches, which all residents were required by law to support and attend.

In 1636, Roger Williams, a young Puritan minister, was banished from the Massachusetts Bay Colony for telling his congregation that no government had the right to tell a person how to worship. Forced worship is false worship, he said. With twelve followers, Williams fled south into the wilderness.

He was welcomed by Narragansett Indians, who gave him enough land to establish the first European settlement in what is now the state of Rhode Island. Grateful for his escape from Massachusetts, Williams named the tiny settlement Providence, "God's Guidance," and there put his ideas about religious liberty to the test. Rhode Island became a haven for religious minorities that were persecuted elsewhere in the colonies.

In Puritan Massachusetts, only church members could vote or hold public office. Those who questioned the church's teachings were, like Williams, exiled to the wilderness, or worse. Quakers in Boston were being executed for their beliefs as late as 1661.

Forced to leave Massachusetts in 1636, Roger Williams found asylum
among the Narragansett Indians. *Rhode Island Historical Society*

In Virginia and other southern colonies, the Church of England was
the official religion, established by law and supported with public taxes.
Catholics, Baptists, and Jews could be fined, jailed, or whipped for practicing
their religion.

But the religious landscape of America was changing. As settlers arrived
from all over Europe, the variety of religious faiths grew. On the eve of the
Revolutionary War, the colonies boasted 749 Congregational churches,
485 Presbyterian, 457 Baptist, 406 Anglican (Church of England), 328
Dutch or German Reformed, 240 Lutheran, and 56 Catholic. There were

Anne Hutchinson, shown here preaching in her house in Boston, was another Puritan religious leader banished from Massachusetts because of her radical views. In 1638, she moved with her family to Aquidneck in what became Rhode Island.
The Library of Congress

also 200 Quaker meetinghouses and 5 Jewish synagogues. Roger Williams's "lively experiment" promising religious liberty was gradually being introduced elsewhere. Pennsylvania, founded by William Penn as a refuge for his fellow Quakers, had become another religious sanctuary and by the late 1700s was home to more than 400 different religious groups.

With so many faiths flourishing in the colonies, laws favoring one religion or another were widely ignored or, at times, resisted. Some Baptists chose to go to prison rather than pay taxes to support another church. In practice, nonbelievers often were exempt from such taxes, but for the Baptists and others, this wasn't enough. They did not regard religious freedom as a *favor* to be granted by the government. They insisted on the *right* not to be taxed to support someone else's religion.

Meanwhile, colonists who feared for their political liberties at the hands of England's Parliament also worried that Parliament might take away their religious liberty. John Adams recalled the "universal alarm against the authority of Parliament," and the foreboding that "bishops, and dioceses, and churches, and priests, and tithes, were to be imposed on us by Parliament.... If Parliament could tax us, they could establish the Church of England with all its creeds . . . and prohibit all other churches."

People throughout the colonies came to believe that true religious liberty required the government to stay out of religion completely—to neither

Puritans on their way to church. Painting by G. H. Boughton. *The Library of Congress*

support nor oppose religious practices of any kind. For if government authorities had the power to promote religion, then they also had the power to suppress it.

After independence, while the United States remained primarily a Protestant country, it had become a remarkably tolerant place compared to other nations. In 1786, Virginia proclaimed complete religious freedom, ending state support for the Anglican church and guaranteeing every citizen the freedom to worship in any house of prayer. By then, most of the states welcomed members of all Protestant faiths, while some also tolerated Catholics, Jews, and atheists.

The authors of the Constitution decided that tolerance wasn't enough. "The right of every man is to liberty—not toleration," said one. So they included a provision in the Constitution stating that "no religious test shall ever be required as a qualification" to hold any federal office.

This provision was welcome, but many people felt it was too limited. They wanted a bill of rights, added to the Constitution, that would protect religious liberty in all its forms. The result was the opening clause of the First Amendment:

> Congress shall make no law respecting an establishment of religion, or prohibiting the free exercise thereof.

Thomas Jefferson, the author of the Declaration of Independence and a lifelong fighter for religious freedom, wrote in 1802, when he was president of the United States, that the nation had erected "a wall of separation between church and state."

For a very long time, the First Amendment had little effect on American life. Early in the 1800s, the Supreme Court ruled that the Bill of Rights applied only to the national government, and not to state or local governments. While the First Amendment prohibited *Congress* from favoring one religion over others, state governments were not so restricted. The states were not bound to protect individual rights unless required to do so by their own constitutions or laws. In New Jersey, non-Protestants weren't granted full civil rights until 1844. In New Hampshire, Catholics couldn't vote until 1851.

Finally, in 1868, following the Civil War, the Fourteenth Amendment to the Constitution was adopted. Intended to safeguard the rights of newly freed African Americans, it guaranteed equal protection of the laws to all citizens, wherever they happened to live. It says that "no state shall . . . deprive any person of life, liberty, or property, without due process of law." Over time, the Supreme Court ruled that the liberties protected by the Fourteenth Amendment include all those listed in the First, among them religious liberty.

Today, the separation of church and state at every level of government is an accepted principle of American democracy. However, Americans have never been able to agree on how high that "wall of separation" should be, and the language of the First Amendment doesn't really tell us. As a result, important battles are fought virtually every year over such issues as prayer in schools or the use of government funds to support religious activities. When Americans can't agree on constitutional issues, then it is the role of the federal courts, and ultimately the Supreme Court, to interpret the Constitution.

Soon after its founding, the Supreme Court established the right of *judicial review*—the right to examine laws, compare them to the Constitution, and decide whether they are valid. When it comes to constitutional law, the intent and meaning of the Constitution, the Supreme Court has the last word. Its justices have the power to overrule an act of Congress, a presidential order, or a state or local law if they decide that it violates any part of the Constitution.

For example, does the First Amendment permit the use of public funds, raised through taxation, to help support schools run by religious organizations?

That was the question facing the Supreme Court in 2002, when the justices heard arguments in a landmark case called *Zelman v. Simmons-Harris*. The case concerned a controversial program in Cleveland, Ohio, that allowed parents to withdraw their children from public schools and use government-financed vouchers to pay for tuition at private or religious schools.

While all nine justices normally vote on a decision, usually only one actually writes the opinion that decides the case. If one or more justices disagree with the majority decision, then one of them will write a dissenting opinion. That's what happened in the *Zelman* case.

In a narrow 5-to-4 decision, the justices upheld the use of public money for religious school tuition. Writing for the majority, Chief Justice William H. Rehnquist said that Cleveland's voucher program was "neutral in all respects toward religion," since parents could exercise "genuine choice" in deciding where to use their tuition vouchers, at private secular schools or at church-sponsored religious schools.

The justices who dissented, or disagreed, argued that the use of taxpayers' dollars to support religious schools was a violation of the First Amendment. They pointed out that since the vouchers didn't pay enough to cover private school tuition, nearly all students covered by the program used their vouchers at religiously affiliated schools. Once enrolled in those schools, they were required to attend religious services, while tax money went to buy Bibles, prayer books, and other religious items.

Justice John Paul Stevens, a dissenting justice, wrote: "Whenever we remove a brick from the wall that was designed to separate religion and government, we increase the risk of religious strife and weaken the foundation of our democracy."

The role of prayer in the public schools has been another subject of impassioned debate. For much of American history, students at many, perhaps most, public schools were required to start the day by bowing their heads

During the 1960s, the role of prayer in public schools became a controversial First Amendment issue.
The Library of Congress

and reciting a prayer led by teachers. Children whose families did not share the beliefs expressed in those prayers had little choice. They were expected to bow their heads along with their classmates.

Some parents began to object that public-school-sponsored prayer amounts to an "establishment of religion," forbidden by the First Amendment. Then the parents of ten students challenged a New York State law that allowed school officials to require a daily teacher-led classroom prayer. Their case, called *Engel v. Vitale*, wound up before the Supreme Court in 1962. To many people's surprise, the Court sided with the parents. By a vote of 7-to-1, the justices struck down the New York State law, ruling that organized prayer in public schools violated students' First Amendment right to worship as they please.

The ruling was welcomed by those who believed it was wrong to have any form of government-sponsored religious exercise in public schools. And it was condemned by devout believers, who viewed the decision as an insult to prayer and to religion in general.

Justice Hugo L. Black, writing for the Court, rejected the charge that the ruling expressed hostility toward religion. On the contrary, he emphasized that the Court's decision reflected respect for religion and for the great diversity of religious belief in America. Justice Black pointed out that the First Amendment was intended to guarantee that the power of government would never be used "to control, support, or influence the kinds of prayers the American people can say."

When asked to comment on the ruling, President John F. Kennedy—the first Catholic ever to be elected president—agreed with the Court. The most meaningful place for prayer, he said, was in the home and in the church, rather than being imposed on children in public schools.

Since then, the Supreme Court, in other cases, has continued to uphold the constitutional ban on organized classroom prayer, even if the prayers are nondenominational (not of any particular religion) and even if students aren't required to participate. One parent argued that forcing his children to stand in the hallway while their classmates prayed carried the stigma of "punishment for bad conduct."

In a 1992 decision called *Lee v. Weisman,* the Supreme Court also banned prayer led by a member of the clergy at a graduation ceremony. Justice Anthony M. Kennedy, a devout Catholic and a former altar boy, wrote that the Constitution "forbids the State to exact religious conformity from a student as the price of attending his or her own high school graduation."

None of these decisions suggests that students can't say prayers in public schools, alone or in groups, as long as their activities do not disrupt the school or interfere with the rights of others. The Constitution simply prohibits school officials from leading organized prayers. Public schools must neither promote nor discourage religion, the courts have said, and must remain neutral among religions and between religion and non-religion.

Lawmakers, meanwhile, have introduced dozens of constitutional amendments in Congress that would allow prayer in public schools. One congressman said that he wanted to overturn those Supreme Court decisions that have "attacked, twisted, and warped" the First Amendment. So far, none of these measures has received enough votes to pass. Supporters

Supreme Court Justice Hugo L. Black wrote the landmark 1962 ruling that public-school-sponsored prayers are an unconstitutional establishment of religion. Black served on the Court from 1937 to 1971.
The Library of Congress

of the amendments argue that the question of school prayer should be decided by each local community, by a majority of the people concerned, and not by any federal court. Opponents say that the Bill of Rights protects the religious freedom of everyone and that a majority of citizens should never be able to impose their religious preferences or beliefs on a minority.

"The very purpose of the Bill of Rights," said the Supreme Court in 1943, was to place certain rights "beyond the reach of majorities and government officials. . . . One's right to life, liberty, and property, to free speech, a free press, freedom of worship and assembly, and other fundamental rights may not be submitted to a vote; they depend on the outcome of no elections."

What happens when a person's religious beliefs conflict with his or her duties as a citizen? Can an individual who is conscientiously opposed to killing refuse to serve in the military during time of war?

Congress has always provided for some religious exemptions from military service. During both the Civil War and World War I, members of certain religious groups were excused from the draft laws. As conscientious objectors, they claimed that their beliefs forbade them from taking part in war. At the beginning of World War II, Congress laid down stricter rules for religious exemption: to be excused from combat, you had to demonstrate your belief in a traditional religion, one that believes in a personal God, and you had to oppose all wars "in any form," not just a particular war.

However, those rules seemed to discriminate among religions, a conflict that was resolved by the Supreme Court during the Vietnam War. A young man named Donald Seeger had refused induction into the army on religious grounds, even though he belonged to no particular religious group. In 1965, in *United States v. Seeger,* the Supreme Court ruled that belief in God or in a traditional religion wasn't necessary to be classified as a conscientious objector. If the applicant could show that his conscientious opposition

An antiwar demonstrator burns his draft card outside Selective Service headquarters in Northampton, Massachusetts, as part of a nationwide antidraft campaign during the Vietnam War. *AP/Wide World Photos*

to war was based on a "purely ethical creed" that played a major role in his life, then he could be exempted.

Another difficult First Amendment question concerns conflicts between religious freedom and the government's responsibility to protect the health, safety, or general well-being of society at large. Suppose an individual claims that his or her religion forbids vaccination against communicable diseases?

The Supreme Court answered that question back in 1905, ruling in favor of the government: vaccinations can be required if there is a substantial danger to the community. But if only the individual's own health or life is at risk, that person has the right to refuse a vaccination, a blood transfusion, or any other medical procedure that doctors believe can save his life.

This freedom applies only to adults, however. Jehovah's Witnesses, for example, are opposed to blood transfusions on religious grounds. The courts have ruled that adult Witnesses have the right to refuse a life-saving transfusion for themselves. But they cannot refuse transfusions for a child whose life is in danger. In such extreme circumstances, say the courts, religious beliefs can be overridden to protect the life of a child, who did not choose those religious beliefs and is not old enough to make that choice. Opponents of the rulings say that ordering medical treatment for a child whose parents believe that such treatment is against the will of God is a threat to religious freedom.

In most cases in recent times, the courts have acted to protect the rights of religious minorities. Which brings us back to Marie and Gatha Barnett, the Jehovah's Witness sisters who refused to salute the flag. In 1940, the Supreme Court had ruled against the Witnesses, saying that local authorities had the right to set school policies. But the Court often changes its mind on constitutional issues, and that is what happened in the case of the Barnett sisters.

On Flag Day, June 14, 1943, during the darkest days of World War II, the Supreme Court issued its landmark decision in the case of *West Virginia Board of Education v. Barnette* (the name was misspelled in court records). The justices upheld the claims of Jehovah's Witnesses and struck down the state's requirement that students must salute the flag and recite the Pledge of Allegiance at the beginning of each school day. One of the things the

In a 1943 ruling, Supreme Court Justice
Robert H. Jackson defended
the rights of Jehovah's Witnesses and
all other religious minorities to
observe their deeply felt spiritual
convictions. Jackson served on the
Court from 1941 to 1954.
The Library of Congress

Muslims pray at the
Masjid Al-Abidin place
of worship in the
Queens borough
of New York City,
September 14, 2001.
AP/Wide World Photos

flag stands for, said the Court, is the right *not* to salute it. Marie and Gatha were allowed to return to school, half a year behind their classmates. The Court did not prohibit patriotic ceremonies, such as classroom flag salutes, but said that students may be excused if those ceremonies conflict with their religious beliefs.

Writing for the Court, Justice Robert H. Jackson expressed an enduring principle of the Bill of Rights: "If there is any fixed star in our constitutional constellation, it is that no official, high or petty, can prescribe what shall be orthodox in politics, nationalism, religion, or other matters of opinion or force citizens to confess by word or act their faith therein."

In separating church and state, the authors of the Bill of Rights sought to encourage both religion and religious liberty. James Madison, who wrote the First Amendment, said many times that religion would flourish more freely "without the aid of Government."

And that is essentially what has happened. In a world torn apart by religious and ethnic conflict, the United States today enjoys more religious diversity and freedom than perhaps any other country.

THE FIRST AMENDMENT

PART TWO

Congress shall make no law . . . abridging the freedom of speech,
or of the press; or the right of the people peaceably to assemble,
and to petition the Government for a redress of grievances.

4. Freedom of Expression

"Under our Constitution, there is no such thing as a false idea."
—*Supreme Court, 1974*

In December 1965, a group of teenagers in Des Moines, Iowa, wanted to express their opposition to America's involvement in the Vietnam War. They decided to wear black armbands imprinted with a white peace symbol during the holiday season—a statement of protest and an expression of mourning for the dead on both sides of that deeply divisive conflict. When principals at the teenagers' schools learned about the plan, they banned the otherwise peaceful protest as a "disruptive influence."

Most of the students agreed to remove their armbands before going to school every morning. But three refused: thirteen-year-old Mary Beth Tinker; her fifteen-year-old brother, John; and their sixteen-year-old friend, Christopher Eckhardt. When they showed up in class still wearing their armbands, they were suspended from school.

Backed by their parents, and represented by lawyers from the American Civil Liberties Union, the students sued the school district for violating their First Amendment right to freely express their opinions. Their case, *Tinker v. Des Moines Independent Community School District*, made its way through the court system and finally reached the United States Supreme Court.

In 1969, the Court ruled 7-to-2 in the students' favor, declaring that their armbands were a legitimate form of "symbolic speech," protected by the First Amendment. School officials have every right to make school rules and control student conduct, the justices said, but they can't prevent students from exercising *their* right to free expression. Since the armbands did not "materially and substantially disrupt the work and discipline of the school," the students should not have been prohibited from wearing them.

"It need hardly be argued that neither students nor teachers shed their constitutional rights to freedom of speech or expression at the schoolhouse gate," wrote Justice Abe Fortas. "Students in school as well as out of school are 'persons' under our Constitution."

The ruling marked the first time that free expression rights were extended to students at school. But those rights aren't unlimited. In another important case, *Hazelwood School District v. Kuhlmeier,* the Court held that school officials may place reasonable restrictions on students' free-speech rights as long as they have a good educational reason for doing so.

That case involved a group of journalism students at Hazelwood East High School near St. Louis, Missouri. They brought suit because their principal refused to allow the school newspaper to publish two articles that discussed some students' experiences with pregnancy and with divorces in their families.

This time, the Court backed the principal. In 1988, the justices ruled that because the newspaper was published by the school and was part of the journalism curriculum—the students were graded on their stories—the principal could censor any story he considered unsuitable. Since he

Mary Beth Tinker and her brother, John, display the armbands they wore to protest the Vietnam War.
Corbis / Bettmann

Tammy Hawkins, editor of the Hazelwood East High School newspaper, *Spectrum*, holds a copy of the paper in 1988, following the Supreme Court ruling that school officials have broad powers of censorship over student newspapers.
AP/Wide World Photos

believed that the articles in question were inappropriate for some younger students at the school, he had a good reason for censoring them.

Justice William Brennan Jr. disagreed. He said that school newspapers deserved the same protections as the regular press. "The young men and women of Hazelwood East High School expected a civics lesson," he wrote, "but not the one the Court teaches them today."

★ ★ ★

In colonial America, as in England, criticism of the government was called "seditious libel," and it could get you into a whole lot of trouble. People were fined, jailed, or exiled for speaking out against the king or his appointed colonial governors.

The case of John Peter Zenger became famous. Zenger was a German immigrant who published the *New-York Weekly Journal,* the colonies' first politically independent newspaper. In 1735, he was jailed for his stinging criticism of New York's colonial governor, William Cosby. He was held in jail for months before he was allowed to see a lawyer, but still, he would not be silenced. His wife continued to publish the *Weekly Journal.*

At the time, seditious libel was understood to mean *any* damaging criticism of an official, true or false. When Zenger was finally put on trial, his volunteer lawyer, Andrew Hamilton, offered a groundbreaking defense. Hamilton argued that criticism of the government should not be considered libelous if it happened to be *true.* He persuaded the jury that truth should be a defense, and that Zenger's criticisms of Governor Cosby were in fact true. The jury returned a verdict of not guilty.

Zenger and his lawyer were hailed as heroes, and their celebrated case helped establish the principle of press freedom. Gouverneur Morris, one of the men who drafted the Constitution, called the Zenger trial "the germ of American freedom—the morning star of that liberty which subsequently revolutionized America."

After the Revolution, Americans believed that they had the right to express their opinions freely, without interference from the government. That freedom, along with religious liberty, was guaranteed by the First Amendment.

And yet in 1798, just seven years after the Bill of Rights was adopted, Congress did exactly what the First Amendment says it must not do. At a time when war with France threatened, Congress passed the Sedition Act, which made it a crime to "write, print, utter, or publish . . . any false, scandalous, and malicious" comments about government officials, Congress, or the president.

The government now had the power to squelch criticism by hauling into court anyone it wished to silence. Although the Sedition Act allowed

ABOVE:
Picture Collection, The New York Public Library

RIGHT:
British officials burn copies of Peter Zenger's *New-York Weekly Journal* on Wall Street in New York City in 1734. Zenger's criticism of the colonial government landed him in jail.
The Library of Congress

Zenger's trial in 1735 helped establish the principle of press freedom.
Picture Collection, The New York Public Library

for "truth" as a defense, President John Adams's political opponents found that it wasn't easy to prove what was true and what was false. Political truth was a matter of opinion. Dozens of American citizens were tried, convicted, and imprisoned under the law, among them newspaper editors who had criticized the president, and even a congressman, Representative

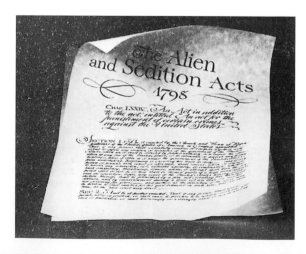

The Alien and Sedition Acts of 1798
(a facsimile).
*Picture Collection, The New York
Public Library*

Matthew Lyon of Vermont, who had opposed the Sedition Act in a letter to a Vermont newspaper.

After Adams lost the presidential election in 1800, the Sedition Act expired, and the new president, Thomas Jefferson, pardoned all those who had been convicted. Congress passed no further sedition laws for more than a century.

In 1917, the United States entered World War I—once known as "the war to end all wars." Just as fear of war with France had prompted the nation's first sedition law in 1798, World War I led to new federal laws restricting freedom of speech. Seeking to ensure wartime patriotism and loyalty, Congress passed the Espionage Act, which made it a crime to interfere with military recruitment or encourage "disloyal" acts. The Sedition Act, passed a year later in 1918, outlawed speech that criticized the United States government or showed disrespect for the flag.

More than two thousand people were prosecuted under these laws, and many were sentenced to long prison terms, mostly for making statements condemning the war. One man, Charles T. Schenck, was arrested for handing out leaflets that urged young men to resist the military draft. He was convicted of violating the Espionage Act.

Schenck appealed his case to the Supreme Court. In *Schenck v. United States*, he argued that the Espionage Act denied him his First Amendment right to freely express his antidraft convictions. The Court disagreed. In a landmark ruling that would influence federal court decisions for years to come, Justice Oliver Wendell Holmes wrote that since the United States was at war when Schenck urged draft resistance, his words had endangered the nation. Drawing a comparison to "falsely shouting fire in a theater and causing a panic," Holmes said that Schenck's wartime leaflets posed "a clear and present [or immediate] danger that they will bring about the substantive evils that Congress has a right to prevent"—such as riots, crimes, or other harm.

Navy Secretary Josephus Daniels, blindfolded, draws a capsule containing a number in the World War I draft lottery, which selected men between the ages of eighteen and forty-five for military service. Charles Schenck was one of many Americans who opposed compulsory enrollment, called *conscription* or the *draft*. *The National Archives*

This decision was viewed by many as a defeat for free speech. It seemed to mean that people could be imprisoned simply for expressing their opinions—for advocating, or supporting, an unpopular cause without actually committing a violent or lawless act. Charles Schenck had distributed a leaflet calling the draft unconstitutional and urging people to peaceably "assert your rights." But he hadn't tried to incite a riot, or shut down a draft board office, or forcibly obstruct the draft. No criminal conduct had taken place as a result of his leaflet. He had been convicted for his words alone, but in 1919, the Supreme Court unanimously upheld his conviction.

That year, federal agencies launched a campaign to rid the country of foreign-born radicals, including members of the recently organized Communist party. Attorney General A. Mitchell Palmer, aided by his young assistant, J. Edgar Hoover, ordered a mass roundup of actual and alleged "Reds." In November 1919 and January 1920, hundreds of FBI agents raided thirty-three cities and arrested, often without warrants, more than four thousand suspected subversives, most of them bewildered immigrants. Many were held for weeks or months without access to lawyers or their families before being deported, sentenced to prison, or released.

The so-called Palmer Raids were supported by many of the nation's newspapers. "There is no time to waste on hairsplitting over infringement of liberty," said the *Washington Post*. But the government's actions stirred protests by civil rights advocates, including future Supreme Court justice Felix Frankfurter, and by the newly formed American Civil Liberties Union, which issued a report condemning the "utterly illegal acts which

On June 16, 1917, five thousand women tried to present an antidraft petition to New York's mayor. Several of the women were arrested when they refused to disperse without seeing the mayor. *The National Archives*

have been committed by those charged with the highest duty of enforcing the laws." Stung by the ACLU report, Attorney General Palmer accused his critics of being "soft" on communism.

Supreme Court Justice Holmes, meanwhile, had been having second thoughts about his ruling in the *Schenck* case. Late in 1919, he felt compelled to revise his "clear and present danger" test and to issue a ringing defense of free speech. He now declared that only the imminent danger of harm, or proof of criminal intent to bring about such harm, can justify setting a limit on the free expression of ideas. Words alone are not enough. "I think we should be extremely vigilant against attempts to check the expression of opinions that we loathe," said Holmes, "unless they so imminently threaten immediate interference with the lawful and pressing purposes of the law that an immediate check is required to save the country."

Supreme Court Justice Louis D. Brandeis joined Holmes in that ruling and as a champion of First Amendment rights. In a succession of important decisions, these two justices upheld the right of Americans to express unpopular ideas. "Those who won our independence believed . . . that freedom to think as you will and to speak as you think are indispensable to the discovery and spread of political truth," wrote Brandeis.

And yet the courts still found it difficult to strike a balance between free speech and the demands of national security. Americans continued to go to

During his thirty years as a
Supreme Court justice, from 1902 to 1932,
Oliver Wendell Holmes Jr. became known as
an eloquent champion of free speech.
The National Archives

jail because of their beliefs and associations. After World War II, there was a period of fierce rivalry between the United States and the Soviet Union known as the cold war. During this time, the Smith Act, passed by Congress in 1940, became a weapon in the government's prosecution of Communist party leaders in the United States. At the time, many Americans believed that the Communist-ruled Soviet Union was determined to take over the world and that American Communists were part of the plan. The Smith Act made it a crime to talk about overthrowing the government by force or violence or to belong to any organization that supported such a belief.

In 1949, eleven Communist party leaders were convicted of violating the Smith Act. They were not accused of any *specific* plot or plan to commit a crime. No evidence of criminal behavior was ever presented. They were convicted solely because of their *association* with the doctrine of communism. In 1951, the Supreme Court upheld their conviction, ruling that the First Amendment does not protect a person who advocates, or supports, the violent overthrow of the United States.

Most of the justices seemed to think that since the Soviet Union was itself a clear and present danger, membership in the American Communist party was also a clear and present danger. Two justices disagreed. Evidently, said Justice Hugo L. Black, only "safe" opinions are protected by the Bill of Rights. The Communist leaders "were not charged with an attempt to overthrow the Government," wrote Black. "They were not charged with overt acts of any kind designed to overthrow the Government. They were not even charged with saying anything or with writing anything designed to overthrow the Government. . . . The indictment is that they conspired to organize the Communist Party and to use speech or newspaper and other publications in the future to teach and advocate the forcible overthrow of the Government."

Between 1951 and 1956, 141 people were indicted under the Smith Act and 29 were sent to prison. And then, in 1957, the Supreme Court reversed itself and struck down the convictions of all defendants. The justices ruled that simply *talking* about overthrowing the government isn't enough. Only if a call to rebellion is accompanied by the urging of a specific lawless *action*—the teaching of techniques of sabotage, the planting of bombs, the assassination of the president—only then may it be forbidden. No further prosecutions were ever brought under the provisions of the Smith Act.

During those cold war years of the 1950s, the loyalty of many Americans was questioned during a massive national campaign to root out suspected Communists from the government and from universities, the press, and the arts. Anyone accused of being a Communist sympathizer was in jeopardy of losing his or her job. For a time, simply holding an unpopular political opinion was enough to taint a person.

The loudest voice in this anti-Communist campaign, often called the Red Scare, was that of Wisconsin Senator Joseph McCarthy. Between 1950 and 1954, McCarthy's name and his unfounded accusations dominated the headlines, creating a climate of political fear and intimidation

Senator Joseph McCarthy covers the microphones with his hands while having a whispered conversation with his chief counsel, Roy Cohn, during a Senate hearing in 1954. *AP/Wide World Photos*

that became known as McCarthyism. Without ever producing the evidence he claimed he had, McCarthy charged that the State Department and other government agencies were harboring scores of undercover Communist agents. He was a master at declaring people "guilty by association," not because they had done anything wrong, but simply because they knew someone or had belonged to a group that others considered suspicious.

McCarthy's tactics quickly turned into an assault against free speech. One of the few public figures who dared to speak out against him was Senator Margaret Chase Smith of Maine, at that time the only woman in the Senate. "I think that it is high time for the United States Senate to do some real soul searching," she said. "The American people are sick and tired of being afraid to speak their minds lest they be politically smeared as Communists or Fascists by their opponents. Freedom of speech is not what it used to be in America."

Finally, McCarthy went too far. A large Senate majority condemned him for his irresponsible accusations, publicly disgracing the senator and putting an end to his power. He died in obscurity of cancer and alcoholism in 1957. But his unscrupulous attacks on free speech and association had destroyed the careers and reputations of innocent people all over the country.

Since the 1950s, the Supreme Court has acted to strengthen First Amendment protections. By 1969, the Court had ruled that the amendment protects *all* speech advocating a cause or idea, no matter how unpopular, unless it is intended to produce, and is likely to produce, a specific and immediate criminal act. The Court has said, in effect, that the government does not have the power to decide which political ideas should be permitted and which should not.

Can burning an American flag be a permissible exercise of free speech? In three separate cases—in 1969, 1989, and 1990—the Supreme Court struck down as unconstitutional laws that prohibited flag burning. The Court ruled that burning a flag is protected by the First Amendment as an expression of political protest, another form of "symbolic speech." The flag stands for the right to free speech, said the Court, and for the right to express anger at the government.

Few Supreme Court decisions have caused a greater outcry. George H. W. Bush, who was president in 1990, was so outraged that he wanted to amend the Bill of Rights. He became the first American president in two hundred years to call for a constitutional amendment that would create an exception to the First Amendment. That exception would have allowed Congress to make it a crime to "desecrate" the flag. After a spirited debate broadcast to the entire nation on television, Congress failed to approve the amendment, and the Bill of Rights remained unchanged.

Another controversial issue concerns so-called hate speech—speech expressing hatred or prejudice toward others because of

A masked Seattle protester burns an American flag moments after a federal flag-burning law went into effect in October 1989. A few months later, the law was declared unconstitutional.
AP/Wide World Photos

their race, religion, national origin, gender, or sexual orientation. The courts have ruled that freedom of expression means equal freedom for everyone—including those with opinions that many people find deeply offensive. It means that the First Amendment protects the expression of prejudiced ideas and beliefs, no matter how false and misguided those beliefs might be.

If false ideas were not protected by the Bill of Rights, then who would decide which ideas are false and which are true? Would we give the government the power to determine which opinions to protect and which to punish? That's why the Supreme Court declared in 1974 that "under our Constitution, there is no such thing as a false idea." Truth and falsity must be decided in the court of public opinion, and not by government decree.

Like all rights, freedom of expression is a right with limits. It doesn't mean that one person has the right to threaten or harass another, or to use words in a manner likely to result in force or lawless behavior. A threatening phone call in the middle of the night is not protected by the First Amendment. Neither is slander (deliberately saying something untrue to damage a person's reputation) or libel (actually publishing false and malicious words or pictures about a person).

Freedom of speech is put to its toughest test when that right is claimed by people who speak out of hatred for others. In 1977, members of the American Nazi party—admirers of the Nazi leader Adolf Hitler—announced that they were planning to march in Skokie, Illinois, a town with a large Jewish population, including thousands of Holocaust survivors, men and women who had survived Nazi death camps. The Skokie town council refused to issue a permit for the march and went to court to try to stop it.

When the American Civil Liberties Union agreed to defend the right of the Nazis to march, thousands of ACLU members resigned in angry protest. And yet the ACLU frequently represents controversial clients as part of its mission to protect all the freedoms promised by the Bill of

A member of the American Nazi party gives the Nazi salute to a crowd of anti-Nazi protesters during a demonstration and counterdemonstration in Chicago's Lincoln Park in 1982. Some thirty Nazis and more than a thousand anti-Nazi demonstrators were separated by a fence and a special detachment of police.
AP/Wide World Photos

Rights. The organization's volunteer lawyers do not necessarily agree with their clients' ideas, but they strongly support each individual's right to freely express both popular and unpopular beliefs.

A federal court ruled that by trying to stop the march, the Skokie town council had violated the Nazis' right to free speech. "Public expression of ideas may not be prohibited merely because the ideas are themselves offensive to some of their hearers," said the court.

The judges pointed out that it is *un*popular speech that needs the protection of the First Amendment. Speech that reflects the views of the majority is rarely suppressed or punished. And so the town council's ban on the march was struck down. By then, the case had aroused such a furor that the Nazis had decided not to march after all.

Many First Amendment issues remain unresolved today. Is "obscenity" a category of speech protected by the Bill of Rights? And who has the right to decide exactly what obscenity is or precisely how to define it? Can the creators of art, books, plays, films, or song lyrics be prosecuted on grounds of obscenity? The courts have agreed that "obscene" material should not be imposed on children or on unwilling adults, but they have not been able to come up with a clear definition of obscenity that is acceptable to everyone.

Should violence on television be restricted? What about vulgar, sexist, or racist rock or rap lyrics? Can a rap group be prosecuted for using "obscene" lyrics? Can record store owners be prosecuted for selling those recordings? In 1990, the rap group 2 Live Crew was prosecuted for using "obscene" lyrics in their album *As Nasty as They Wanna Be*. However, a jury found the group not guilty. "You take away one freedom," a juror said, "and pretty soon they're all gone."

Does the First Amendment protect commercial speech, such as TV commercials, or ads in print, or junk e-mail, also known as spam? Do advertisers—cigarette companies, for instance—have a constitutional right to make any statement or claim they wish? Should bulk e-mailers be required to label spam honestly, so that recipients can filter it out or choose not to receive it?

Should school and public libraries remove books from shelves that some people object to on political, religious, or other grounds? Books of all kinds are constantly being challenged in communities around the United States. Among the many books some parents have wanted to remove from libraries for one reason or another are Mark Twain's *The Adventures of Huckleberry Finn*, Katherine Paterson's Newbery Medal–winner *Bridge to Terabithia*, Laura Ingalls Wilder's *Little House on the Prairie*, and *The Diary of Anne Frank*.

Author Kurt Vonnegut speaks on book banning and censorship at the New York office of the American Civil Liberties Union, October 3, 1980. The books in front of him, including his own *Slaughterhouse-Five*, were removed from school libraries by the Island Trees, New York, school board.
AP/Wide World Photos

In a 1982 case concerning school-library censorship, the Supreme Court ruled against the Island Trees, New York, school board, which had removed nine books from the library on grounds that they offended community values. In *Board of Education, Island Trees Union Free School District No. 26 v. Pico,* the Court held that students' rights were violated by removal of the books and said that a school library provides "an environment especially appropriate for the recognition of First Amendment rights of students."

School officials have a great deal of power to decide which books should be in their school libraries, but they "may not remove books from school library shelves simply because they dislike the ideas contained in those books," said the Court. "Allowing a school board to engage in such conduct hardly teaches children to respect the diversity of ideas that is fundamental to the American system."

★ ★ ★

And what about the worldwide computer network known as the Internet—a medium of communication that the authors of the Bill of Rights could scarcely have imagined? Can the government restrict what you see and read on-line?

In 1996, Congress passed the Communications Decency Act, which made it illegal to send, transmit, or display "indecent" or offensive material to children under eighteen years of age. A year later, the Supreme Court struck down the law, declaring that First Amendment protections clearly apply to the Internet. The justices recognized the government's interest in protecting children. But they ruled that the law as written was too vague and too broad. Since it was impossible to determine at any given time who

Members of the Harvest Assembly of God church throw books, CDs, and videos into a "holy fire," March 25, 2001, in Butler, Pennsylvania. Harry Potter books and the works of Shakespeare were among the items considered "satanic deceptions" and burned in church bonfires in 2001. *AP/Wide World Photos*

was on-line and how old that person was, the Court found that the law would unnecessarily limit speech addressed to adults.

To overcome these objections, Congress has attempted to restrict Internet use through other laws, each of which has been challenged. The Children's Internet Protection Act, passed in 2001, would require public schools and libraries to block Internet sites "harmful to minors" by installing software programs called filters. Critics of the act say that the filtering technology that libraries would have to use is highly unreliable, because it also blocks many unobjectionable sites.

Even if Internet filters could be made more accurate, opponents say, the act would be unconstitutional because the filters do not distinguish between adults and minors, which means that adult library patrons would be denied access to material. The law was still being debated in the federal courts in 2002 and was expected to be decided by the Supreme Court.

Meanwhile, the Internet continues to raise other questions even as it revolutionizes communications. Is there a constitutional right to send junk e-mail that can overload computer systems? Are chat room or system operators responsible for untrue statements published on the Internet? Do schools have the right to control what students write on-line?

The questions are endless. But the key question, as always when it comes to freedom of expression, is: Who decides?

"First Amendment freedoms are most in danger when the government seeks to control thought," Supreme Court Justice Anthony M. Kennedy has said. "The right to think is the beginning of freedom, and speech must be protected from the government because speech is the beginning of thought."

THE SECOND AMENDMENT

A well-regulated Militia, being necessary to the security of a free State, the right of the people to keep and bear Arms, shall not be infringed.

5. The Right to Bear Arms?

"To preserve a free state today, perhaps the people must be 'armed' with modems more than muskets."
                                                        —*Akhil Reed Amar*

It's been called "the embarrassing Second Amendment," "the murky Second," and "the orphan of the Bill of Rights." And it's been hailed as the very cornerstone of the United States Constitution. For years, the Second Amendment has been the storm center of a ferocious national debate about gun control and individual rights.

Perhaps because so many guns already are in circulation, most people, according to polls, believe that the Second Amendment gives individuals a personal right to own guns. So far, however, the courts have tended to rule otherwise. The Supreme Court has said that the amendment merely guarantees a *collective* right to arms—by "well-regulated" state militias or by National Guard units—and extends no such right to individuals.

The United States is the only industrialized country that allows widespread possession of guns. It has been estimated that half or more of all American homes contain at least one gun. The United States also suffers from a far greater death rate from both deliberate and accidental shootings than any other advanced country.

In America today, one person dies by gunshot every eighteen or nineteen minutes, twenty-four hours a day. That added up to 28,874 deaths in 1999, down from 30,708 the year before. During a typical two-year period, more Americans are killed by guns here at home than were killed during the entire Vietnam War.

A handgun training class for women, Macoupin County, Illinois, 1981.
Corbis / Bettmann

American children in particular face a greater risk from guns than the children of any other industrialized nation. In one recent year, firearms killed no children in Japan, 19 in Great Britain, 57 in Germany, 109 in France, 153 in Canada, and 5,285 in the United States.

The Second Amendment begins with the words "A well-regulated Militia." In colonial America, each colony had its own militia—a military force made up of ordinary citizens serving as part-time soldiers. All able-bodied men between the ages of sixteen and fifty or sixty, depending on the colony, were required to serve. The men elected their own officers and were expected to furnish their own muskets, bullets, and gunpowder. They met on training days to perform military maneuvers and stay acquainted with handling guns. They thought of themselves mainly as an armed guard ready to defend their homes and localities, not as manpower for wars.

When the Revolutionary War began, George Washington had to rely on the state militia units until he could raise a professional fighting force. And yet he felt that the militiamen were poorly trained and unreliable. As emergency soldiers, summoned from home on short notice, they lacked confidence on the battlefield. Discipline was lax. Desertions were commonplace.

"To place any dependence on militia is assuredly resting on a broken staff," Washington told Congress early in the war. "Men, just dragged from the tender scenes of domestic life, unaccustomed to the din of arms, totally

A colonial militiaman prepares for war. *The Library of Congress*

Minutemen fire at British troops on Lexington Green, April 19, 1775.
The Library of Congress

unacquainted with any kind of military skill . . . are timid and ready to fly from their own shadows. Besides, the sudden change in their manner of living brings on an unconquerable desire to return to their homes, and produces the most shameful and scandalous desertions."

As the war progressed, Washington and his generals used the militia as auxiliary troops around a core of regulars from the Continental Army. Led by experienced officers, and with the regular army to support them, the militiamen often fought bravely and won some victories without the help of the Continentals.

After the war, the U.S. Constitution established a permanent professional army made up of full-time soldiers, controlled by the national government. But with the memory of King George III's British troops still fresh in mind, the early Americans distrusted any standing army "as the instrument of tyrants and the enslaver of peoples."

The authors of the Bill of Rights wanted to protect the independence of the state militias, which could act as a safeguard against federal tyranny. If the national government ever abused its powers and sent the army to seize control from the states, then the states' "well-regulated" militias would be standing by to help defend the people's liberties. After much discussion and many changes of wording, the Second Amendment was written to prevent the national government from disarming the state militias.

At first, local militia units were used to put down local rebellions by citizens and to suppress uprisings by slaves. But as the nation grew, the militia system faded away, until it was no longer a national institution. Citizen militias as the early Americans knew them do not really exist today. The so-called militias of our own day are actually small private armies of self-styled superpatriots, white supremacists, and other heavily armed groups that harbor a vehement dislike of the American government and the conviction that an unarmed population can be easily enslaved.

Private armies have never been the method most Americans have favored to keep our democratic government responsible and sensitive to the needs of the people. "To preserve a free state today," writes constitutional scholar Akhil Reed Amar, "perhaps the people must be 'armed' with modems more than muskets, with access to the Internet more than the shooting range." Referring to the democratic movements in Russia and China in the late 1980s, he said, "Fax machines are perhaps the most powerful weapons of all."

Until fairly recent times, people didn't pay much attention to the Second Amendment. But with the spiraling increase in gun violence in America, "the right of the people to keep and bear arms" has come under intense scrutiny.

Supporters of strict gun-control measures contend that the right to bear arms is limited by the Second Amendment's preamble, its opening clause:

LEFT:
Flathead County Sheriff Jim Dupont displays weapons and ammunition being held as evidence in an alleged plot by a militia group to assassinate law enforcement officers and local officials, Kalispell, Montana, February 15, 2002.
AP/Wide World Photos

BELOW:
David Burgert (center with beard), head of the militia group, being booked on assault charges by Kalispell, Montana, police. He is wearing a "2nd Amendment" T-shirt with a picture of a Revolutionary War minuteman.
AP/Wide World Photos

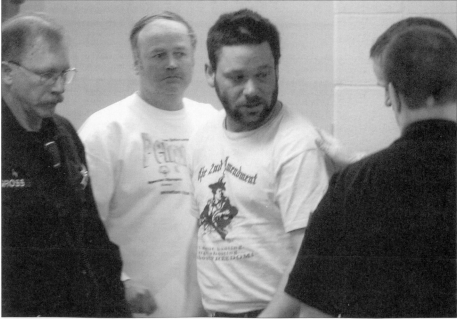

"A well-regulated Militia, being necessary to the security of a free State." They argue that the amendment guarantees a collective right to arms by members of state militias or today's equivalent, the National Guard, rather than any personal right to carry a weapon. And they demand legislation to limit the sale and possession of firearms, especially handguns.

Opponents of gun control claim that the Second Amendment gives every citizen a nearly absolute right to own guns for self-defense and for private pursuits like hunting and target shooting. They argue that gun-control laws violate their Second Amendment rights and do little to reduce or prevent gun-related violence. "We think [the Second Amendment] means no gun control and that all gun-control laws are unconstitutional," says Larry Pratt, director of the 300,000-member Gun Owners of America.

So whose right to bear arms is it—the state's or the individual's?

In 1939, in a landmark case called *United States v. Miller,* the Supreme Court ruled that the "obvious purpose" of the Second Amendment was to "assure the continuation and render possible the effectiveness" of the state militias. Unless the owner of a firearm could demonstrate "some reasonable relationship to the preservation and efficiency of a well-regulated militia" or "that its use could contribute to the common defense," then possession of a weapon, said the Court, was not protected by the Second Amendment. By viewing the amendment as a collective rather than an individual right, the Court's ruling left room for broad gun ownership regulation.

Since then, the Supreme Court and most lower federal courts have continued to interpret the Second Amendment as protecting only the right of state-organized militias to own firearms. "The very language of the Second Amendment refutes any argument that it was intended to guarantee every citizen an unfettered right to any kind of weapon," according to former Supreme Court Chief Justice Warren Burger. "Surely the Second Amendment does not remotely guarantee every person the constitutional right to have a 'Saturday Night Special' [a cheap handgun] or a machine

National Guardsmen
stand guard following
riots and looting in
Los Angeles,
August 17, 1965.
The Library of Congress

gun without any regulation whatever. There is no support in the Constitution for the argument that federal and state governments are powerless to regulate the purchase of such firearms."

Demands for strict gun-control measures were spurred by the 1981 shooting of President Ronald Reagan and his press secretary, James Brady, which led to the passage of the Brady Law by Congress. That measure required background checks on certain handgun purchases and a waiting period before a purchaser could take possession of a gun. In 1989, after a man firing a semiautomatic rifle killed five California schoolchildren, the federal government banned the import of most foreign-made assault rifles. However, in 1999, following the massacre of twelve students and a teacher at Columbine High School in Littleton, Colorado, pro-gun lobbyists and their allies in Congress managed to stop any further expansion of existing firearms regulations.

Recent court decisions have shown how difficult it is to put this controversial issue to rest. In 2001, a federal appeals court in New Orleans ruled that "the Second Amendment *does* protect individual rights" to possess firearms, but added, "That does not mean that those rights may never be made subject to any limited, narrowly tailored specific exemptions." In 2002, however, a federal appeals court in San Francisco seemed to take the contrary view. That court held that the amendment protects only the *collective* right of state-organized militias and National Guard units to own firearms. Judge Stephen Reinhardt argued that "there exists no thorough judicial examination of the [Second] Amendment's meaning" and described the Supreme Court's 1939 ruling on the gun-ownership issue as "somewhat cryptic."

President Bill Clinton signs the Brady Bill into law as James Brady looks on, November 1993. Brady was shot and permanently disabled in John Hinckley's attempted assassination of President Ronald Reagan in 1981. Reagan, also shot, made a full recovery.
Corbis / Bettmann

So far, no gun-control measure has ever been declared unconstitutional on Second Amendment grounds. Constitutional scholars Laurence H. Tribe and Akhil Reed Amar have pointed out that "almost no right known to the Constitution is absolute and unlimited—not even the rights of free speech and religious exercise." The First Amendment protects free speech, for example, but does not entitle a person to falsely yell "Fire!" in a crowded theater or to commit libel or perjury. "The right to bear arms," say Tribe and Amar, "is certainly subject to reasonable regulation in the interest of public safety. Laws that ban certain types of weapons, that require safety devices on others, and that otherwise impose strict controls on guns can pass constitutional scrutiny."

Opposition to gun-control measures has long been a political rallying cry of the National Rifle Association, a powerful lobbying organization with more than three million members. Officials of the NRA have opposed most gun control measures. They argue that regulation of firearms can lead to the confiscation of all guns in private hands. And they say that gun control is the first step toward the government taking away all rights. Gun control laws will not stop criminals from getting guns illegally, the gun lobby argues, while law-abiding citizens need guns for self-protection.

Supporters of gun control say that nothing in the Second Amendment restricts Congress or the states from regulating the possession and use of guns. They point out that guns in the hands of private citizens are often more dangerous than the criminals those guns are intended to repel. And they plead that something must be done about the escalating epidemic of gun violence that has resulted in the assassination or attempted assassination of three recent presidents, drive-by shootings, school shoot-outs, and thousands of American deaths every year.

Demands for stricter gun-control laws took on an increased urgency following the September 11, 2001, terrorist attacks against the World Trade Center in New York City and the Pentagon in Washington, D.C. Several lawmakers announced that they would try to close the so-called gun-show loophole in the Brady Law and require the same background checks at gun shows that are mandatory when someone buys a firearm from a licensed dealer at a store.

"Our current gun laws are so weak that our country serves as a virtual arsenal for terrorists," said California Representative Henry Waxman. He noted that even .50 caliber sniper weapons, with the capacity to shoot down helicopters and pierce bunkers, can be had for the asking at gun shows.

National Rifle Association president Charlton Heston addresses gun owners during a "get-out-the-vote" rally in Manchester, New Hampshire, October 21, 2002. *AP/Wide World Photos*

"Guns and Terror," a report issued by the Brady Center to Prevent Gun Violence, called the United States "The Great Gun Bazaar." The report noted that manuals for potential terrorists include instructions on how to use weak U.S. laws to obtain firearms legally.

The NRA, urging its backers to prepare for another political battle over gun control, said, "The war on terrorism will not be won by attacking the rights of American citizens."

THE THIRD AMENDMENT

No Soldier shall, in time of peace be quartered in any house,
without the consent of the Owner, nor in time of war,
but in a manner to be prescribed by law.

6. The Right to Be Left Alone

Uninvited Guests

"This provision speaks for itself." —Justice Joseph Story

Suppose that you answer your front door one morning and are informed by an army officer that several soldiers, who are complete strangers, are going to be staying with you—whether you like it or not. You and your family will have to make room for them. And besides putting them up, you'll also be expected to feed them.

As unlikely as that may seem in the twenty-first century, it has been a common practice in some parts of the world and was a source of anger and resentment in the American colonies of the 1770s. In the years leading up to the Revolutionary War, the British stationed large numbers of troops in the principal colonial towns. To accommodate these redcoats, as the soldiers were called, the English Parliament passed a series of Quartering Acts.

The first act took effect in 1765. It required each colony to provide barracks for the British troops and supply them with free food, bedding, firewood, cooking utensils, and a daily allowance of cider. A second Quartering Act, passed a year later, decreed that if enough barracks weren't available, then the troops must be housed in livery stables, public inns, and alehouses.

When members of New York's colonial assembly objected, the British authorities suspended the assembly's right to pass laws of any kind. The New York assemblymen finally gave in and agreed to obey the Quartering

Acts. They voted funds to house and feed the redcoats, but ill feelings persisted on both sides.

In 1774, following the Boston Tea Party, rising tensions between the colonists and the British led to a strict new Quartering Act. This time, soldiers were to be put up in private homes, as well as in commercial buildings. Although the colonists protested bitterly, the new law was enforced and unwilling Americans now had British soldiers sitting at their dinner tables and sleeping in their beds. "It is downright and intolerably wrong!" one colonist complained.

Boston, a town of some sixteen thousand, was occupied by five thousand British troops. Many of the soldiers camped in tents on Boston Common, and yet it seemed that almost every house in town had unwelcome redcoat lodgers.

The quartering of British troops in America demonstrated to the colonists the dangers and abuses of standing armies. They felt that the

A woodcut by Paul Revere shows the landing of British troops
in Boston in 1768. *The Library of Congress*

An artist's impression of British troops entering Boston in 1768. *Culver Pictures*

"absolute tyranny" of England's King George III had now reached right into their own homes. And so when Thomas Jefferson wrote the Declaration of Independence in 1776, he listed as two of the colonists' chief grievances against the king, and as reasons for rebellion, keeping "among us, in time of peace, Standing Armies, without the Consent of our legislatures" and "quartering large bodies of armed troops among us."

By the time the Bill of Rights was written and approved, the Revolutionary War had long since ended, the defeated British army had gone home, and the quartering of troops in private homes was no longer a burning issue. Even so, the early Americans could not be certain what a powerful federal government might do in the future. With the Third Amendment, they intended to make sure that Congress could never conscript civilians as involuntary innkeepers and roommates of soldiers in peacetime.

In 1833, a Supreme Court justice named Joseph Story summed up the Third Amendment: "This provision speaks for itself. Its plain objective is to secure the perfect enjoyment of that great right of the common law, that a man's house shall be his own castle, privileged against all civil and military intrusion. The billeting of soldiers in time of peace upon the people has been a common resort of arbitrary princes, and is full of inconvenience and peril."

The Third Amendment was meant to protect civilian values against the threat of an overbearing military. It was an expression of the early Americans' distrust of standing armies and their abiding belief, inherited from centuries of English tradition, that "a man's house is his castle."

So far, it has never been necessary to invoke the Third Amendment. The American military has never felt the need to commandeer people's homes. However, the amendment hasn't been forgotten. In recent years, the Third, along with other amendments, has been called upon to support the idea of a constitutional right to privacy.

For if soldiers have no right to intrude upon your home, then does any government agent have that right?

THE FOURTH AMENDMENT

The right of the people to be secure in their persons, houses, papers, and effects, against unreasonable searches and seizures, shall not be violated, and no Warrants shall issue, but upon probable cause, supported by Oath or affirmation, and particularly describing the place to be searched, and the persons or things to be seized.

7. The Right to Be Left Alone

Searches and Seizures

"The right to be left alone—the most comprehensive of rights and the right most valued by civilized men."
—*Justice Louis D. Brandeis*

Early one morning, the police show up without warning to search your home. They're going to empty every closet, pull out every desk and bureau drawer, take every book from your shelves, read your private letters and papers—all on the chance that they might find evidence of wrongdoing or disloyalty.

That's what happened in Nazi Germany under Adolf Hitler and in the Soviet Union under Joseph Stalin. It happens today in totalitarian countries around the world. And it happened in colonial America.

During the 1700s, British soldiers and customs inspectors invaded homes, shops, and offices at will. Armed with warrants called writs of assistance, they searched any person or place they chose, often with no better reason than a vague suspicion, a rumor, or a whisper from an informer. Usually they were looking for smuggled goods, but they also carried out searches to punish political opposition and squelch dissent.

The colonists recognized the need for police to search for evidence of criminal behavior. But they resented the practice of government agents barging in to nose around whenever they pleased, even when they had no evidence of a violation. This unlimited authority to search was seen as a

Die Americaner wiedersetzen sich der
Stempel Acte, und verbrennen das aus
England nach America gesandte Stempel-
Papier zu Boston. im August 1764.

Unrestricted searches of
homes and offices were one
of many grievances
that led to anti-British riots
in the American colonies.
This German etching
depicts an uprising in
Boston in 1764.
The Library of Congress

threat to the colonists' liberties, an attack on the traditional right to privacy
claimed by every British subject who believed that his house was his castle.

That right was defended by the British statesman William Pitt in a
speech to Parliament in 1763, when he opposed a bill authorizing general

searches: "The poorest man may, in his cottage, bid defiance to all the forces of the Crown. It may be frail; its roof may shake; the wind may blow through it; the storm may enter; the rain may enter; but the King of England may not enter; all his forces dare not cross the threshold of the ruined tenement."

Despite his eloquence, Pitt did not convince his fellow members of Parliament. The hated practice of unlimited searches continued in the American colonies despite determined and sometimes violent resistance. One angry colonist, a Boston merchant, barricaded his house and refused entry to customs inspectors while a crowd gathered outside and cheered him on.

At a Boston town meeting in 1772, the colonists expressed their rage: "Thus our houses and even our bed chambers, are exposed to be ransacked, our boxes chests & trunks broke open ravaged and plundered by wretches, whom no prudent man would venture to employ even as menial servants. . . . Flagrant instances of the wanton exercise of this power, have frequently happened in this and other seaport towns."

British sympathizers in the rebellious American colonies were sometimes strung up and ridiculed, as shown in this 1795 engraving.
The Library of Congress

After the Revolution, there was a strong public demand to prohibit such searches forever. That demand resulted in the Fourth Amendment, which was intended to allow reasonable searches and ban unreasonable ones. The original American citizens insisted that no search should be authorized unless the government could show specific reasons for suspecting a particular individual of a criminal act. The right to be secure in one's own home meant that not even the highest government official could enter the humblest household without a court order based on adequate evidence.

The Fourth Amendment has two requirements. Before a search can take place, the police must furnish evidence that a crime has occurred and that the person or place to be searched is likely to contain evidence of that crime. This is known as *probable cause*. The second requirement is that the decision to authorize a search must be made not by the police themselves but by an impartial judge who, if satisfied by the evidence, will then issue a *search warrant*. Evidence that is seized illegally, in violation of the Fourth Amendment, cannot be used against an accused person in criminal court.

An important exception involves a search that takes place during an arrest, which happens to be when most searches are conducted. A person can be stopped and frisked by the police if they think they have a good reason, and the person can be thoroughly searched if the police go ahead and make an arrest. As a rule, no warrant is necessary so long as the search is confined to the arrested person and his or her immediate surroundings.

When the Fourth Amendment was written, a search always meant an actual physical examination of a person's belongings, letters, and papers. The early Americans could not foresee the sophisticated spying devices available to police officers today. Wiretapping and electronic eavesdropping were unknown back in 1791. When they first began to appear, the courts had a hard time deciding if and when the Fourth Amendment restricted their use.

Los Angeles police search one of several suspects arrested for selling narcotics, April 9, 1988. *AP/Wide World Photos*

Wiretapping was a brand-new technique during the 1920s, the era of alcohol prohibition in the United States. A suspected bootlegger named Roy Olmstead was convicted of selling liquor illegally after police placed phone taps in the basement of his office building and on wires in the streets near his home. Olmstead appealed his conviction, arguing that the wire-taps were a search conducted without a warrant and without probable cause. The evidence against him should have been thrown out, he claimed, because it was gathered illegally.

Prohibition officers raid a Washington, D.C., lunchroom in search of illegal stocks of liquor, April 25, 1923. During the period of national Prohibition, from 1920 to 1933, the manufacture and sale of alcoholic beverages was prohibited in the United States. *The Library of Congress*

When his case, *Olmstead v. United States,* reached the Supreme Court in 1928, the justices rejected his arguments on the grounds that no physical entry of his home or office had taken place. By a 5-to-4 vote, the Court ruled that the government has the power to wiretap without any Fourth Amendment restrictions.

Justice Louis D. Brandeis disagreed. In his famous and often-quoted dissent, he said that both the Fourth and Fifth Amendments were meant to protect an individual's privacy, which he defined as "the right to be left alone—the most comprehensive of rights and the right most valued by civilized men. To protect that right, every unjustifiable intrusion by the Government upon the privacy of the individual, whatever the means employed, must be deemed a violation of the Fourth Amendment."

Brandeis warned that the "progress of science in furnishing the Government with means of espionage" would make it much more difficult to protect the right of privacy. And he said that electronic methods of eavesdropping would make the Fourth Amendment meaningless unless those methods were subject to the same restrictions as an actual physical search.

His fellow justices were not persuaded, however, and for nearly forty years, the Court's ruling in the *Olmstead* case meant that wiretapping and electronic eavesdropping were not limited by the Fourth Amendment. But eventually, the Supreme Court reversed the *Olmstead* decision. In 1967, the justices ruled 8-to-1 that wiretapping, after all, is an unconstitutional invasion of privacy, except in limited circumstances. Warrants based on specific evidence of criminal behavior are now required before wiretaps can be authorized, just as with an actual physical search.

Since then, the courts have been challenged by a host of new questions raised by rapidly changing law-enforcement technology. What exactly is a search? At what point does the Fourth Amendment begin to apply? Can your home remain your castle in an age when high-tech devices can hear and virtually see right through your walls?

Supreme Court Justice Louis D. Brandeis warned in 1928 that electronic methods of eavesdropping endangered the constitutional right to individual privacy. Brandeis served on the Court from 1916 to 1939.
The Library of Congress

In 2001, the Supreme Court considered a technological marvel that the Constitution's framers most certainly did not have in mind: a thermal imaging device that the police can use from outside a home to detect patterns of heat being generated inside. The question before the Court was whether the use of a thermal imager by the police is a search that, no less than actual entry into a house, requires a warrant.

This case involved an Oregon man, Danny Lee Kyllo, who was convicted of growing marijuana in his home. In his appeal, Kyllo argued that the police had conducted an illegal search by using a thermal imager to detect heat being generated by high-intensity lights employed for marijuana cultivation. Sitting in a parked car, the police determined that Kyllo had turned his home into a marijuana hothouse. They then used that information to get a warrant to actually enter and search the house, where they found more than a hundred marijuana plants growing under halide lights.

In this contest between old-fashioned personal privacy and newfangled law-enforcement technology, the winner was privacy. The Court ruled 5-to-4 in *Kyllo v. United States* that the police need a warrant to aim a thermal imaging device at the outside walls of a house, just as they need a warrant to enter that house. The justices added that the warrant requirement applied not only to the heat-sensing device in question but also to any "more sophisticated systems" in use or development that let the police gain knowledge that in the past would have been impossible to obtain without entering the home.

Justice Antonin Scalia declared that the Court would not "leave the homeowner at the mercy of advancing technology," which someday may be able to discern all activities inside a house. "The Fourth Amendment draws a firm line at the entrance to the house," said Scalia. "That line, we think, must be not only firm but bright."

Another question raised by advancing technology concerns an individual's private papers and records. The early Americans normally kept their personal records at home or at a place of business. Today, personal information that would have been considered private in 1791 is often kept by someone else. The story of your life can be found in your school records, in banking and hospital records, in telephone company records that register every phone number you dial, and in credit card transactions that detail every book you buy, every movie you rent, every trip you take.

The Supreme Court has ruled that because these records are not in our own custody, we don't really expect privacy. For that reason, personal information in a database kept by someone else isn't protected by the Fourth Amendment, and the government doesn't need a search warrant when it wants to look. To some extent, privacy rights in this area have been protected by state and federal laws rather than by the Bill of Rights.

In the past, the Fourth Amendment hasn't always been an effective barrier against unfounded government snooping. For decades, former FBI director J. Edgar Hoover used wiretaps and other electronic devices to spy on thousands of political figures and other citizens not even suspected of committing crimes—among them, critics of the Vietnam War and leaders of the civil rights movement. Martin Luther King Jr. was the target of persistent

Writing for the Supreme Court in 2001, Justice Antonin Scalia declared that despite advancing technology, people in their homes should have the same level of privacy that existed when the Fourth Amendment was adopted in 1791. Scalia was appointed to the Court in 1986.
The Library of Congress

eavesdropping between 1963 and 1966. The FBI placed wiretaps on his home and office phones and planted concealed microphones, or "bugs," in many of the hotel rooms where King stayed as he traveled across the country.

Congress outlawed this practice in 1968, banning warrantless wiretaps and requiring specific evidence of criminal behavior before a wiretapping warrant could be issued. An exception was allowed in cases involving "national security," but in 1978, Congress attempted to close this loophole by passing the Foreign Intelligence Surveillance Act, which required warrants

A Massachusetts State Police officer watches as his bomb-detecting German shepherd sniffs a passenger's luggage at Boston's Logan International Airport, July 26, 1996. Most people accept warrantless airport searches—passing through metal detectors, putting luggage through X-ray machines, submitting to personal searches—in the interests of safety and security. *AP/Wide World Photos*

Security guards search a car entering the Rockefeller Center parking garage in New York, following the February 26, 1993, car bomb attack at the World Trade Center garage. *AP/Wide World Photos*

for national-security as well as for criminal cases. The act established a special Foreign Intelligence Surveillance Court, which reviews eavesdropping applications by federal agencies and issues warrants in secret proceedings.

Most recently, following the September 11, 2001, terrorist attacks in New York City and Washington, D.C., the U.S. Justice Department announced that it would monitor all conversations between certain people in federal custody (mostly for immigration violations) and their lawyers. The Department said that information gained from such electronic eavesdropping might help prevent future terrorist acts, even though it would not be admissible as evidence in court.

This policy provoked an outcry from civil liberties groups and from some members of Congress. They complained that the new eavesdropping regulation clearly violated constitutional guarantees of the right to counsel and the right to be free of unreasonable searches. Conversations between an attorney and a client, like those between a doctor and a patient, or a priest and a parishioner, have always been considered confidential, or privileged, which means that a person cannot be forced to divulge what was said. Senator Patrick J. Leahy, the chairman of the Senate Judiciary Committee, said that the government should devise ways to counter terrorists without losing "the freedoms we are fighting to protect."

In 1980, two high school students in New Jersey were caught smoking in a school bathroom. One admitted the offense and was suspended for three days. The other, a fourteen-year-old girl, denied the charge. An assistant principal searched her purse and found a pack of cigarettes, some rolling papers, a bag of marijuana, and lists of names, suggesting that she was selling the drug. The school called the police, and the girl was suspended for ten days.

When her case came up in juvenile court, she was charged with delinquency based on possession of marijuana with intent to sell. Her parents filed suit, challenging both the delinquency charge and the school suspension on grounds that her Fourth Amendment rights against "unreasonable searches and seizures" had been violated.

The case, called *New Jersey v. T.L.O.* (the girl's name was never released), reached the Supreme Court in 1985. The justices ruled that students are indeed protected by the Fourth Amendment—but not to the same extent as adults. Since teachers and administrators must maintain discipline and order in the classroom and on school grounds, they are not subject to the same strict standards as the police.

School officials don't need a warrant from a judge to search a student. All they need is a "reasonable suspicion" that something illegal is going on, not the "probable cause" called for by the Fourth. They must conduct the search in a "reasonable" way, based on the student's age and sex and what they are looking for. And they must suspect that a particular individual has broken a law or a school rule, not just "someone." Just because they suspect that *some* students have broken the law doesn't give them the authority to search *all* students. So in the case of *T.L.O.*, the Court held that the assistant principal's search of her purse was both lawful and reasonable.

A more recent Supreme Court decision dealt with random drug-testing programs, in which school officials test several students or perhaps an entire class because they suspect that someone—but nobody in particular—is taking drugs. A drug or alcohol test is considered a search under the Fourth Amendment.

James Acton, with friends and family members, leaves the Supreme Court in Washington, D.C., after Acton's hearing on mandatory drug testing, March 28, 1995. From left are Kathy Armstrong of the American Civil Liberties Union, Acton's brother Simon, James, and his parents, Judy and Wayne. *AP/Wide World Photos*

In this case, *Vernonia School District 47J v. Acton,* James Acton was a twelve-year-old seventh-grader who wanted to try out for his school's football team in Vernonia, Oregon, a small logging town where school officials were determined to combat a growing drug problem. A mandatory drug test—a urine sample collected in school—was required of all students who wanted to join the football team.

James's parents refused to sign a consent form for the test. They felt that the school had no reason to suspect that James, a model student, was taking drugs. And they claimed that the test, to be conducted with a male teacher standing behind James, was an unreasonable search of his body and an unconstitutional invasion of his and their privacy. The responsibility for drug testing, they insisted, rested with them, not with the school board.

In 1995, the Supreme Court ruled 6-to-3 against James, who was by then sixteen. The Court found that drug use among students in the school district had become a major problem. And it held that students gave up at least part of their right to privacy when they joined athletic teams—for example, by regularly undressing and showering together.

The justices concluded that the benefits of drug testing outweighed any invasion of privacy. Public schools, they said, can require random drug testing of student athletes whether or not they are suspected of using drugs, suggesting that the key issue in this case was not privacy rights but deterring drug use. As to James's claim that the urine test was intrusive and embarrassing, Justice Antonin Scalia said, "School sports are not for the bashful."

Justice Sandra Day O'Connor disagreed. While she supported the idea of random drug testing, she argued that the actions of the Vernonia school officials amounted to a mass, suspicionless search that was, on its face, unreasonable. It would have been "far more reasonable," she said, for the school to limit testing to those students who could reasonably be suspected of taking drugs.

The Court's decision was hailed by some as another way of combating drug use among America's young people. It was condemned by civil rights advocates, who argued that it made students second-class citizens and sacrificed individual rights on the altar of the drug war. Meanwhile, the decision left open the possibility that other students, not just athletes, might also be subject to random drug testing. And in fact, that's what happened in 2002, when the Supreme Court expanded its ruling in the *Acton* case.

In this new case, *Board of Education v. Earls,* the justices voted 5-to-4 to uphold a program at a school in Tecumseh, Oklahoma, that required random drug testing of students engaged in any "competitive" extracurricular activity, including the cheerleading squad, the choir, the band, and the Future Homemakers of America. Students who refused would not be allowed to take part in these school activities.

The Tecumseh program was challenged by Lindsay Earls, an honor student, after she was called out of choir practice to submit to a urine test that

Sandra Day O'Connor was one of three Supreme Court justices who dissented in the *Acton* case. In 1981, she became the first woman appointed to the Court.
The Library of Congress

Dartmouth College freshman Lindsay Earls of Tecumseh, Oklahoma, challenged her high school's program of random drug testing, required of all students taking part in extracurricular activities. In 2002, the Supreme Court ruled against her.
AP/Wide World Photos

she considered an invasion of privacy. Lindsay passed her drug test but, with the backing of her parents, persisted in her court challenge. She had graduated from Tecumseh High and was a freshman at Dartmouth College by the time the case reached the Supreme Court, which ruled in favor of random drug testing.

THE FIFTH AMENDMENT

No person shall be held to answer for a capital, or otherwise infamous crime, unless on a presentment or indictment of a Grand Jury, except in cases arising in the land or naval forces, or in the Militia, when in actual service in time of War or public danger; nor shall any person be subject for the same offence to be twice put in jeopardy of life or limb; nor shall be compelled in any criminal case to be a witness against himself, nor be deprived of life, liberty, or property, without due process of law; nor shall private property be taken for public use, without just compensation.

8. The Right to Remain Silent

"I was condemned because I would not accuse myself."—John Lilburne

On a wintry morning in the year 1638, John Lilburne, a twenty-three-year-old clothier's apprentice, stood before the dreaded judges of the Royal Star Chamber in London, England. Lilburne had been jailed for distributing political pamphlets. The judges ordered him to take a solemn oath: he must swear on the Bible that he would truthfully answer all questions put to him.

Lilburne refused, fearing that he might be forced to incriminate himself or others. He insisted that the oath violated his rights under the "law of the land" and the Magna Carta. "I am not willing to answer," he said, "because I see you go about this examination to ensnare me; for seeing the things for which I am imprisoned can not be proved against me, you will get other matter out of my examination."

He would not take the oath even "though I be pulled to pieces by wild horses."

The judges held Lilburne in contempt of court and fined him five hundred pounds. As he was taken in an open wagon from the courtroom to his prison cell, he was publicly whipped, raising two hundred bloody welts on his back. Then he was placed in solitary confinement until such time as he should agree to take the oath—potentially a life sentence. "I was condemned," he later wrote, "because I would not accuse myself."

In England at the time, laws made it a crime to call the king a fool, to predict his death, or to damage his reputation in any way. It was also a crime to circulate literature or perform plays that criticized or made fun of

The names of the Jury of life and death

John Lilburne's twenty-year battle for fair trial procedures made him known throughout England as a symbol of individual rights. This 1649 engraving is titled "The Names of the Jury of Life and Death." *Picture Collection, The New York Public Library*

the established church or expressed opinions that conflicted with official church doctrine. Those laws were enforced by special courts called the High Commission, which judged crimes against the church, and the Star Chamber, the highest government court. Offenders were dealt with harshly. They might be sentenced to have their ears cut off, their cheeks branded, their noses slit, or their bodies whipped.

Individuals could be brought before the High Commission or the Star Chamber without any formal charges, and without being informed of the accusations against them or the identities of their accusers. They had no right to be represented by a lawyer. The judges themselves tried the case, determined guilt, and imposed the sentence, without the inconvenience of a jury.

If a person failed to confess, the court might extract a confession by torture—the fastest and most efficient way to get at the "truth," as some judges believed. Interrogators might encourage the accused by crushing his thumbs, pulling out his nails, or stretching him on the rack until his bones broke and the confession came. Innocent people were sometimes tortured into confessing "crimes" they knew nothing about.

In time, torture was replaced by the solemn "oath *ex officio*," which required accused individuals to answer any questions that might be asked—such as "Who were your accomplices when you plotted against the king?" The questions were intended to establish their guilt of certain crimes, though they were not always told what those crimes were. If they took the

The medieval rack—on which the victim's body was stretched by ropes attached to the limbs—was one of several instruments of torture used to extract confessions. According to Amnesty International, many countries today still use torture against captured enemies, rebels, political opponents, and human rights activists. *Picture Collection, The New York Public Library*

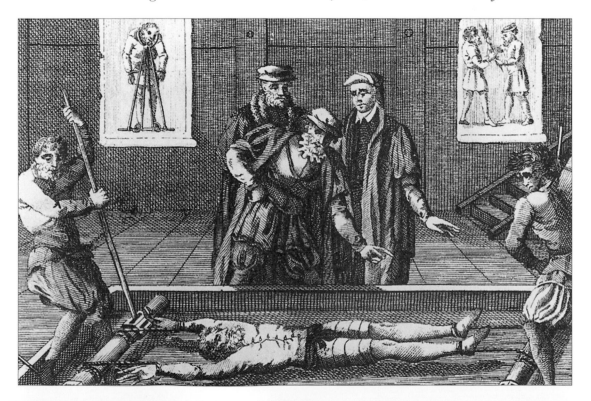

oath and answered truthfully, they could be punished for religious or political crimes they didn't even know they had committed. If they tried to protect themselves by lying, they could be punished for perjury. And if, like John Lilburne, they refused to take the oath, they could be held in contempt and thrown into prison, which often meant a slow and cruel death.

Lilburne's defiant courage made him a popular hero. His insistence on fair treatment focused England's attention on the injustice of the nation's court proceedings. And his willingness to suffer for his principles helped bring about the abolition of the feared and hated Royal Star Chamber in 1641.

That year, Parliament prohibited any oath that required a person "to confess or to accuse himself or herself of any crime." The Star Chamber proceedings were declared to be "bloody, wicked, cruel, barbarous, and tyrannous." Lilburne's sentence was reversed, he was released, and he was awarded damages for his unjust imprisonment. Even then, he continued to campaign against injustice and was arrested several more times for his political views. He died in prison in 1657, at the age of forty-three.

Lilburne became known throughout England as "Freeborn John." His dogged twenty-year battle for fairness convinced his fellow citizens that those accused of a crime should never be forced to testify against themselves. More than any other individual, he helped reform England's judicial system and establish rights that guarantee fairness when a person is accused of a crime.

By the time the Bill of Rights was adopted in America, a century and a half later, the right to remain silent was accepted without question in both England and the United States. That fundamental right had been written into the constitutions of eight of the original thirteen states. It became a key provision of the Fifth Amendment:

> No person . . . shall be compelled in any criminal case to be a witness against himself.

Of all the amendments, the Fifth is the most varied. It spells out several rules concerning the rights of an individual accused of a "capital" or "infamous" crime—a crime that can be punished by imprisonment or death.

To begin with, the amendment provides for a grand jury, a panel of citizens that holds hearings to determine if there is enough evidence that a crime has taken place to justify a trial, in which case a regular jury would decide innocence or guilt. This prevents the government from prosecuting a person when it has little or no evidence of guilt.

The Fifth says that no one can be tried for the same offense twice—that's called double jeopardy—unless legal errors have been committed during the first trial. This prevents the government, with all its resources and power, from persecuting an individual by subjecting him or her to the ordeal and expense of repeated trials.

The amendment requires "due process of law," that is, a fair hearing or trial before an accused person can be deprived of "life, liberty, or property." And it assures "just compensation," a fair price, if the government takes over private property for public use.

The one provision of the Fifth that has caused plenty of controversy is the right to remain silent when accused of a crime. Television courtroom dramas often feature trial scenes in which a witness takes the stand and announces: "I refuse to answer on the grounds that it may incriminate me." Newspapers print headlines about witnesses who "take the Fifth," such as COMPANY EXECUTIVE PLEADS FIFTH AT SENATE INQUIRY or CITY OFFICIAL DECLINES TO TESTIFY AT GRAFT HEARINGS.

Critics of this provision ask why an innocent person would refuse to answer questions. If an individual has nothing to hide, why not agree to testify instead of resorting to the Fifth?

The authors of the Fifth Amendment knew that innocent people accused of crimes are sometimes wrongly convicted. They understood that a witness in a criminal trial can be intimidated or confused into answering

A television camera films the courtroom during a murder trial in Waco, Texas, December 7, 1955. This is believed to be the first murder trial ever televised in the United States. The arrow points to the defendant, Harry Washburn.
The Library of Congress

incriminating questions. Under sharp and persistent questioning, an innocent person who is trying to tell the truth may unwittingly give testimony that helps a prosecutor prove a case against that person.

Current methods of DNA testing have revealed that this happens all too often. In recent years, hundreds of men and women have been released from prison, some of them from death row, because DNA tests have proven that they could not possibly have committed the crimes for which they were convicted. Many of these hapless but innocent people had been forced or tricked or bullied into confessions, including confessions of murder, or had unwittingly testified against themselves in a courtroom. According to the

Innocence Project at the Cardozo School of Law in New York, false confessions have played a role in twenty percent of all DNA exonerations.

The right to remain silent was written into the Bill of Rights to help ensure fair play for the criminally accused. That right reflects the belief that in a free society, an accused person is innocent until proven guilty beyond a reasonable doubt, and that the burden of proof is on the prosecution.

The biggest controversy involving the Fifth was triggered by a Supreme Court ruling in 1966. Until then, an accused person's right to remain silent or ask for a lawyer wasn't always acknowledged during a police interrogation. Some people in police custody were aware of their rights and knew how to demand them, but many others—those who were poor, unedu-

Film actor Robert Taylor prepares to testify before a Senate committee during the "Red Scare" of the early 1950s. Some witnesses invoked their Fifth Amendment rights and refused to answer questions about their political beliefs and associations. *Stock Montage*

cated, or frightened—felt helpless and intimidated in the back room of a police station.

Ernesto Miranda, a twenty-three-year-old truck driver, had been arrested at his Phoenix, Arizona, home and accused of kidnapping and raping an eighteen-year-old girl, who identified him at the police station. After two hours of questioning, he signed a confession, which was used as evidence at his trial. He was convicted and sentenced to a long prison term.

Miranda's lawyers appealed the verdict on the grounds that the police had not informed him of his rights and had pressured him into signing his confession. Since he was forced to act as a witness against himself, the lawyers said, his confession should not have been used as evidence.

The Supreme Court agreed and threw out Miranda's conviction. In a landmark 5-to-4 decision, the justices ruled in *Miranda v. Arizona* that before police can question suspects, they must inform them of the following: that they have the right to remain silent, that anything they say can be used against them in court, that they have the right to be represented by a lawyer, and that if they cannot afford a lawyer, one will be appointed before questioning, if they so wish.

The Court reached this decision after an extensive review of actual police interrogation practices. The justices found that intimidation and

In 1966, the Supreme Court overturned the conviction of Ernesto Miranda (at right), who had been arrested and interrogated by the police without first being informed of his rights. He is shown here with his attorney, John J. Flynn.
Corbis/Bettmann

**CUSTODIAL INTERROGATION
(MIRANDA) WARNING**

After each part of the following warning, the officer must determine whether the suspect understands what he is being told:

1. You have a right to remain silent. You do not have to talk to me unless you want to do so.

2. If you do want to talk to me, I must advise you that whatever you say can and will be used as evidence against you in court.

3. You have a right to consult with a lawyer and to have a lawyer present with you while you are being questioned.

4. If you want a lawyer but are unable to pay for one, a lawyer will be appointed to represent you free of any cost to you.

5. Knowing these rights, do you want to talk to me without having a lawyer present? You may stop talking to me at any time and you may also demand a lawyer at any time.

even outright physical abuse were common methods of extracting confessions and that the very fact of "custodial interrogation . . . carries its own badge of intimidation."

Speaking for the majority, Chief Justice Earl Warren said that the American "system of criminal justice demands that the government seeking to punish an individual produce the evidence against him by its own independent labors, rather than by the cruel, simple expedient of compelling it from his own mouth." Word for word, Warren dictated the "Miranda warning" that police must now give all suspects to inform them of their rights.

The decision was hailed by civil libertarians as a victory for individual rights, and as protection against possible police brutality and illegally obtained evidence. And it was attacked by conservatives as undermining the efforts of law enforcement officials.

Chief Justice Earl Warren served on the Supreme Court from 1953 to 1969. The Warren Court, as it was known, handed down many important decisions that expanded the rights of citizens.
The National Archives

Four of the nine Supreme Court justices issued a bitter dissent. They predicted that the *Miranda* ruling would tie the hands of the police, shackle law enforcement, and increase the crime rate. Justice Byron White warned that the decision "will return a killer, a rapist or other criminal to the streets" to commit more crimes.

Apparently, that did not happen. According to a 1988 American Bar Association survey, most law enforcement officials felt that the *Miranda* rules have helped ensure fairness and have not been a significant obstacle to law enforcement.

Ernesto Miranda did not return to the streets. Because his first trial was based on inadmissible evidence—his confession—he was able to start over and have a new trial. Jurors in his second trial—who were not allowed to hear his confession—convicted Miranda once again, and he served his prison term.

Miranda was not an idealistic reformer like John Lilburne. Yet his case established the "right to remain silent" under police interrogation. The Supreme Court justices who reversed his first conviction declared that he was entitled to the same rights as any other criminal defendant and that, saint or sinner, the Bill of Rights applies to all.

THE SIXTH AMENDMENT

In all criminal prosecutions, the accused shall enjoy the right to a speedy and public trial, by an impartial jury of the State and district wherein the crime shall have been committed, which district shall have been previously ascertained by law, and to be informed of the nature and cause of the accusation; to be confronted with the witnesses against him; to have compulsory process for obtaining witnesses in his favor, and to have the Assistance of Counsel for his defence.

THE SEVENTH AMENDMENT

In suits at common law, where the value in controversy shall exceed twenty dollars, the right of trial by jury shall be preserved, and no fact tried by jury, shall be otherwise reexamined in any Court of the United States, than according to the rules of the common law.

9. The Right to a Fair Trial

"Under our Constitution, the condition of being a boy does not justify a kangaroo court."
—*Justice Abe Fortas*

During the early Middle Ages, a person accused of a crime might be subjected to a trial by ordeal. An ordeal by fire required the accused individual to walk through fire, or place a hand in a flame, or plunge that hand into molten metal. After several days, someone considered an authority would inspect the burns and decide from their severity the person's innocence or guilt. It was widely believed that Divine Providence would spare an innocent person serious injury.

An ordeal by water might determine if an accused woman was actually a witch. The woman was bound and thrown into a body of water that had been blessed. If she floated, it meant that the water had rejected her, and she was judged guilty. If the blessed water received her and she sank, then she was considered innocent—even if she drowned.

Trial by ordeal in one form or another was an ancient legal custom practiced throughout Europe and in many other parts of the world. In England, such trials were common until the twelfth or thirteenth century, when the ordeal was gradually replaced by the use of the jury, which to the English meant "twelve men, good and true."

Offenses against Church and Crown continued to be tried by judges of the Star Chamber and the High Commission, without juries. But for ordinary criminal and civil trials, the use of the jury and the practice of calling witnesses became an accepted part of England's system of common law—law established by usage and tradition.

In the American colonies, the jury played an important role in protecting ordinary citizens against the tyranny of royal judges and officials. "The institution of the jury . . . places the real direction of society in the hands of the governed . . . and not in that of the government," wrote Alexis de Tocqueville, a French aristocrat who visited the United States in 1831 and wrote the classic study *Democracy in America*.

This old German engraving depicts an ordeal by water, which was thought to determine whether an accused woman was actually a witch.
Picture Collection, The New York Public Library

One of the colonists' biggest grievances was the British use of special courts that did away with juries. Among the many abuses cited in the Declaration of Independence was "depriving us, in many cases, of the benefits of Trial by Jury." That was another injustice that the authors of the Bill of Rights wanted to correct.

Both the Sixth and Seventh Amendments call for jury trials in federal criminal and civil cases. With the Fifth Amendment and the Eighth, they are part of a cluster of rights designed to ensure fair play in criminal proceedings. Taken together, these four amendments promise *due process of law*—a legal phrase that goes back to 1354, when the English Parliament passed a law prohibiting the government from imprisoning anyone "without being brought in answer by due process of law."

Due process means a system of fair procedures that help safeguard a person's legal rights. The Sixth Amendment spells out eight specific rights to which persons accused of a crime are entitled, among them "the right to a speedy and public trial." *Speedy* means that an accused person can't be locked up and held in prison for years without a trial.

A "public trial" prevents the kind of secret inquisition practiced by the Star Chamber, or the secret trials common today in tyrannical countries, where a person can be convicted and imprisoned without anyone knowing about it. Trials in the United States are supposed to be open to the public, which means that anyone can sit in the courtroom and observe the proceedings.

The trial must be heard by an "impartial jury of the State and district wherein the crime shall have been committed." That leaves out everyone with a special interest in the case, such as family members, friends, or associates of either the accused or the prosecution, or anyone with a strong prejudice concerning the issue at hand. The courts have ruled that a jury should reflect a reasonable cross section of the local community. Jurors must be selected without intentionally excluding anyone because of race, religion, income, beliefs, or gender. But this wasn't always the case.

A nineteenth-century jury, made up entirely of white males. From *Harper's Weekly,* February 20, 1869. *Picture Collection, The New York Public Library*

Women weren't allowed to serve on juries until 1920, when they finally won the right to vote. After that, in many states, women could *volunteer* for jury service, but they weren't required to serve until the Supreme Court ruled in 1975 that the "systematic exclusion" of women violated the "fair cross-section requirement" for a jury trial.

In some places, African Americans and Mexican Americans were never called for jury duty until a series of court decisions made it clear that such exclusion violates the Sixth Amendment. In one landmark case, the Supreme Court threw out the conviction of a Mexican-American defendant because no one with a Hispanic name had served on a jury in that Texas county for twenty-five years.

Today, the only people who can be automatically excluded from a jury are those who don't speak English, citizens of a country other than the United States, convicted felons, and the mentally impaired.

While the Sixth Amendment doesn't spell out exactly what a jury should be, the Supreme Court has ruled that in federal criminal cases, a jury should consist of twelve people, and the trial should be supervised by

During the twentieth century, a series of Supreme Court rulings held that juries must reflect a "fair cross-section" of the community, ending the exclusion of women and members of minority groups. This photo shows the jury in a courtroom scene during the filming of *Black Marketeering*, a motion picture produced by the U.S. Office of War Information in 1943. *The Library of Congress*

a judge who can instruct the jurors on points of law. Because the guilt of a defendant must be established beyond any "reasonable doubt," a jury's verdict has to be unanimous. If all twelve jurors can't agree, then a verdict can't be rendered and a new trial may be held. In some states, certain criminal and civil cases are handled by juries with less than twelve members and a unanimous verdict isn't required.

The Sixth Amendment deals with criminal cases. Noncriminal, or civil, cases are covered by the Seventh Amendment, which says that all citizens have a right to a jury trial when they are seeking damages in a lawsuit "where the value in controversy shall exceed twenty dollars." Back in the 1790s, when the amendment was written, twenty dollars was a lot of money, equal to perhaps two weeks' wages for a skilled worker. Today, the Seventh Amendment has succumbed to inflation, and a lawsuit tried in federal court must exceed ten thousand dollars to justify a jury trial.

Along with a "speedy and public trial" and "an impartial jury," the Sixth Amendment says that a defendant must "be informed of the nature and cause of the accusation." In the past, people were often arrested and interrogated without knowing what they had done or said; they might be imprisoned for years with no specific charges being brought against them.

An accused person must have a chance "to be confronted with the witnesses against him" and to challenge and cross-examine those witnesses. It's hard to defend yourself if you don't know who your accusers are. The accused must also have a chance to "obtain witnesses in his favor," people who will testify in his defense.

Finally, the Sixth Amendment promises the accused the right "to have the Assistance of Counsel for his defence"—the right to be represented by a lawyer. Despite this guarantee, legal assistance wasn't available to every defendant until a small-time gambler and odd-jobs man named Clarence Earl Gideon decided to stand up for his rights.

Gideon had been charged with breaking into a pool hall in Panama City, Florida, with the intent to steal money. At his trial, he asked for the aid

Clarence Earl Gideon challenged his Florida
burglary conviction on grounds that he was
too poor to hire a lawyer and the state
refused to supply him with one.
AP/Wide World Photos

Gideon studied law
books in prison, then
sent this handwritten
petition to the
Supreme Court.
The National Archives

No. 490 Misc.

DIVISION OF CORRECTIONS
CORRESPONDENCE REGULATIONS OCT. TERM 1961
U.S. Supreme Court

MAIL WILL NOT BE DELIVERED WHICH DOES NOT CONFORM WITH THESE RULES

No. 1 -- Only 2 letters each week, not to exceed 2 sheets letter-size 8 1/2 x 11" and written on one side only, and if ruled paper, do not write between lines. Your complete name must be signed at the close of your letter. Clippings, stamps, letters from other people, stationery or cash must not be enclosed in your letters.

No. 2 -- All letters must be addressed in the complete prison name of the inmate. Cell number, where applicable, and prison number must be placed in lower left corner of envelope, with your complete name and address in the upper left corner.

No. 3 -- Do not send any packages without a Package Permit. Unauthorized packages will be destroyed.

No. 4 -- Letters must be written in English only.

No. 5 -- Books, magazines, pamphlets, and newspapers of reputable character will be delivered only if mailed direct from the publisher.

No. 6 -- Money must be sent in the form of Postal Money Orders only in the complete prison name and prison number.

INSTITUTION _____

NAME _____

RECEIVED
JAN 8 1962
OFFICE OF THE CLERK
SUPREME COURT, U.S.

In the Supreme Court of the United States
Washington D.C
Motion for leave to proceed in Forma Pauperis
Clarence Earl Gideon, Petitioner
vs.
H. G. Cochran Jr, Director, Divisions of
corrections State of Florida Respondent

Petitioner, Clarence Earl Gideon, who is now
held in the Florida state penitentiary, asks
leave to file the attached petition for a
Writ of Certiorari to the United States
Supreme Court, directed to The Supreme
Court of The State of Florida, without
prepayment of costs and to proceed in
Forma Pauperis. The petitioner's affidavit
in support is attached here-to.
                    Clarence Earl Gideon
                    counsel for Petitioner
Affidavit in support of petition for
leave to proceed in Forma Pauperis
        Clarence Earl Gideon, petitioner
            vs.
H. G. Cochran Jr, Director, Divisions of
corrections State of Florida, Respondent.

I, Clarence Earl Gideon, being duly sworn
according to law, depose and say That I am

of a lawyer, saying that he had no money to hire one on his own. The judge refused on the grounds that Florida law supplied lawyers only in capital, or extremely serious, cases. Gideon was convicted. He was sentenced to eight years in prison.

A high-school dropout, Gideon began to study law in the prison library. Eventually, he sent a petition, handwritten on prison stationery, to the Supreme Court, explaining that he could not afford a lawyer to file the petition for him and asking the Court to review his sentence.

The Court agreed. In 1963, with the help of volunteer lawyers from the American Civil Liberties Union, Gideon won his appeal and the right to a new trial. A unanimous Supreme Court ruled, in *Gideon v. Wainwright,* that the "Assistance of Counsel" called for by the Sixth Amendment is a fundamental right that belongs to everyone, rich or poor. The noble ideal that every defendant stands equal before the law "cannot be realized if the poor man charged with a crime has to face his accusers without a lawyer to assist him," wrote Justice Hugo L. Black.

At his new trial in Florida, Gideon's lawyer demolished the state's evidence against him, proving among other things that Gideon worked part-time at this pool hall and had a key to enter. This time, the jury found him not guilty.

Ever since the *Gideon* decision, poor defendants in criminal trials have been furnished with lawyers. Even so, organizations that offer lawyers for the poor, such as the Legal Aid Society, don't always have the funds they need. And court-appointed lawyers are often overworked and underpaid. They may have little time to prepare cases or meet with their clients. One defense attorney was observed sleeping through parts of his penniless client's murder trial. The accused man was convicted and wound up in a Texas prison on death row.

Another landmark case concerned a minor, fifteen-year-old Gerald Gault. In 1964, Gerald was taken into custody by an Arizona sheriff after a neighbor complained that the boy had made an obscene phone call. In hearings at a detention center, Gerald was never told that he could remain silent, that he could have a lawyer, or exactly what the charges against him were. He had no opportunity to confront or cross-examine the neighbor who accused him. And his parents were never served with a complaint.

Because Gerald was already on probation for an earlier petty theft, he was declared a delinquent in need of protection by the juvenile court. The judge sentenced him to a state reform school for six years, until the age of twenty-one. An adult found guilty of the same offense would have been fined fifty dollars or sentenced to sixty days in jail.

Gerald's parents hired an attorney and challenged the sentence on grounds that the boy had been denied his rights under both the Fifth and Sixth Amendments. By the time the case, called *In re Gault,* reached the Supreme Court in 1967, Gerald had already spent more than two years in reform school. He was finally released when the justices ruled 8-to-1 in his favor.

Minors must receive many of the same constitutional protections as adult defendants, said the Court, including a court-appointed attorney if they need one. "Under our Constitution," wrote Justice Abe Fortas, "the

Abe Fortas waits outside the Senate Judiciary Committee hearing room while the committee considers his nomination to the Supreme Court. Fortas served on the Court from 1965 to 1969. His landmark ruling in the *Gault* case extended to juvenile offenders many (but not all) of the rights of adult criminal defendants.
The Library of Congress

condition of being a boy does not justify a kangaroo court." A "kangaroo court" is an unfair court set up in violation of established legal procedures, usually with the intention of finding a person guilty.

Other court decisions since then have supported the view that minors as well as adults are entitled to the due process rights guaranteed by the Bill of Rights. Minors—young people under eighteen, seventeen, or sixteen, depending on the state—must be informed of the charges against them. They have the right to be represented by a lawyer in criminal cases, the right to remain silent, and the right to confront witnesses who testify against them.

Minors do not always have the right to trial by jury, however. Usually, they are sent to juvenile courts, sometimes called family courts, where hearings are conducted privately by a judge to protect the young offender's identity, rather than being heard by a jury.

Juvenile courts tend to be more lenient than adult courts would be. But when it comes to serious crimes such as murder or rape, officials may choose to prosecute teenagers as adults rather than as juveniles. Instead of being sent to a rehabilitation program or sentenced to time in a juvenile prison, a teenager tried as an adult faces the same severe penalties as an adult. A minor may be too young to vote, to serve on a jury, to legally drink alcoholic beverages, or even to drive, but when juveniles stop acting like children and commit violent crimes, they can be given long terms in adult prisons and even the death penalty.

The protections of the Bill of Rights are most often tested at times of national emergency or war. During the early days of World War II, following the December 7, 1941, Japanese attack on Pearl Harbor, Japanese Americans became the target of widespread prejudice and suspicion, even though there was no evidence of espionage or disloyalty among them. Bending to public and military pressures, President Franklin D. Roosevelt authorized the forced relocation of more than 110,000 people of Japanese

ancestry from their homes on the West Coast to desolate camps sur-
rounded by barbed wire and armed guards.

The internees were never charged with crimes or given a hearing. The
majority were women and children. About two-thirds were native-born

Members of the Mochida family in Hayward, California, wait to board
the evacuation bus that will take them to a World War II detention camp
for people of Japanese ancestry, May 8, 1942. *The National Archives*

American citizens, deprived of their civil liberties. Some were kept imprisoned for three years or more, and many lost their homes, farms, or businesses.

Four decades later, in 1983, a presidential commission reported that the
Japanese Americans had suffered a "grave injustice," brought about by
"race prejudice, war hysteria, and a failure of political leadership." Finally,
Congress passed the Civil Liberties Act of 1988, which offered an unprece-

A Japanese-American child sits with her family's baggage while waiting to be
transported to a relocation center, April 1942.
The National Archives

dented governmental apology and compensation of $20,000, tax-free, to each of the more than 60,000 survivors of the internment camps. "Ancestry is not a crime," said one survivor.

In 2001, following the September 11 terrorist attacks in New York City and Washington, D.C., some twelve hundred foreigners, mainly Arab and Muslim men, were rounded up by the government in a nationwide sweep for possible suspects connected to the attacks. The charges against them, the places they were being held, and, in many cases, their names were kept secret from the public. Most of the detainees had been picked up for minor visa violations or because of neighbors' suspicions.

The government continued to hold some of these men long after their immigration cases were resolved, but failed to indict any of them for terrorist activity. A Justice Department order, meanwhile, allowed officials to conduct warrantless wiretaps of confidential conversations between some of the detainees and their lawyers.

These mass arrests and secret detentions sparked a national debate: Can we find security from terrorist attacks without giving up the constitutional freedoms we are fighting to preserve? The government claimed that the detentions were a necessary precaution, justified by the need for heightened security. Civil rights advocates agreed that the government needed to be cautious. But they argued that holding people indefinitely without charging them with a crime swept aside basic constitutional rights. In the United States, as opposed to tyrannical societies, the government is not permitted to jail people without offering a legally sound reason and without giving the accused an opportunity to challenge their loss of liberty. "Secret arrests," said federal judge Gladys Kessler, "are a concept odious to a democratic society."

The Bill of Rights makes no distinction between citizens and noncitizens. It refers throughout to "the people" or to "persons." The right to a speedy and public trial, to consult with a lawyer beyond the range of government microphones, and to protection against being held in secret for minor crimes are not for Americans alone.

In 1755, Benjamin Franklin reminded his fellow citizens that freedom comes with a high price tag. "Those who would give up essential liberty to purchase a little temporary safety, deserve neither liberty nor safety," he said.

THE EIGHTH AMENDMENT

Excessive bail shall not be required, nor excessive fines imposed, nor cruel and unusual punishments inflicted.

10. Cruel and Unusual Punishment

"For ten years, I felt less than human." —*Ray Krone*

In England during the 1600s, a typical sentence handed down in a treason trial condemned the offenders to be

> hanged up by the neck, to be cut down while ye are yet alive, to have your hearts and bowels taken out before your faces, and your members cut off and burnt, your heads severed from your bodies, your bodies divided into four quarters, your heads and bodies respectively to be disposed of according to the King's will and pleasure; and the Lord have mercy on your souls.

Even when an offender's life was spared, punishment could be gruesome. Alexander Leighton, a Puritan clergyman, was convicted in 1630 of libeling the Church of England. He was fined ten thousand pounds, a staggering sum at the time, and was whipped unmercifully until he was almost dead. Then his head and hands were locked in a pillory, where he was exposed to public ridicule and scorn. One ear was nailed to the pillory and then cut off. His cheek was branded with a hot iron. His nose was slit. A week later, he suffered the same mutilations on the other side of his face. And he was sentenced to prison for life.

In time, people began to complain that the punishments imposed by English courts were "barbarous," "inhuman," "unchristian," and "unjust."

So when the English Bill of Rights was passed by Parliament in 1689, it included a provision that outlawed "cruel and unusual punishment."

Even so, the courts continued to impose punishments that may seem cruel and unusual to us today but in those days were thought to match the crime. Criminals still had their hands, feet, or ears cut off, their nostrils slit, their cheeks branded. Severe floggings were common and continued as punishments in England well into the twentieth century.

In the American colonies, punishments were usually more lenient. While in England women were burned alive for the crime of witchcraft, in America, accused witches were simply hanged. Whipping was the most common

The pillory, a popular form of punishment in colonial America, subjected offenders to public scorn and humiliation. From an 1892 lithograph.
The Library of Congress

ABOVE:
The ducking stool consisted of a chair in which an offender was tied and then ducked repeatedly into water. *Picture Collection, The New York Public Library*

BELOW:
Public whippings were a common punishment during the 1700s.
Stock Montage

punishment in the colonies, along with lesser penalties like the pillory and the ducking stool, which subjected the offender to public humiliation.

In America, as in England, public sentiment prompted several colonies to ban punishments that were considered cruel or excessive. The Massachusetts Body of Liberties, drafted in 1641, declared that "for bodilie punishments we allow amongst us none that are inhumane Barbarous or cruell." By the time the Declaration of Independence was signed in 1776, seven of the original thirteen colonies had banned cruel and unusual punishments. And when the Bill of Rights was written in 1789, the language of the Eighth Amendment was taken word for word from the English Bill of Rights, written a century earlier:

> Excessive bail shall not be required, nor excessive fines imposed, nor cruel and unusual punishments inflicted.

The Eighth is the shortest of all the amendments. It says, in effect, that the punishment should fit the crime.

Bail, of course, is not actually punishment but rather a sum of money a defendant must deposit in order to stay out of jail until the case goes to trial and the jury reaches a verdict. It is a guarantee that the defendant will show up for trial on the date set. The clause banning "excessive bail" was intended to prevent the government from jailing people indefinitely without a trial. In the past, judges had sometimes fixed bail at impossibly high rates, far more than a defendant could hope to raise. As a result, a person accused of a crime but not convicted might languish behind bars for months or years.

Judges had also at times imposed huge fines, requiring payments that could ruin a person convicted of a relatively minor crime—a practice that continues in some countries today as a means of silencing critics of the government. A defendant who couldn't pay the fine might be thrown into debtor's prison and left to rot. To remedy this injustice, the Eighth Amendment banned "excessive fines."

Our understanding of the word "excessive," however, changes with the times. In early America, a $100 fine might represent several weeks' wages.

The meaning of "cruel and unusual punishments" has also changed over time. When the Eighth Amendment was being debated by the First Congress, one member, Samuel Livermore of New Hampshire, objected to the amendment. "It is sometimes necessary to hang a man," he said, "villains often deserve whipping, and perhaps having their ears cut off, but are we in the future to be prevented from inflicting these punishments because they are cruel?"

It was left to future generations to decide just what "cruel and unusual punishments" would mean to them. Public flogging was abolished in America in 1839. But it wasn't until 1910 that the Supreme Court was finally asked to define "cruel and unusual punishments." The Court left it up to public opinion. The Eighth Amendment "is not fastened to the absolute but may acquire meaning as public opinion becomes enlightened by human practice," said the Court.

Today, serious crimes are punished by prison sentences rather than any form of corporal punishment—the infliction of physical pain or discomfort. The courts have outlawed physical punishment in the military services and in mental hospitals and prisons. In a case involving prisoners in Arkansas, a judge ruled that the use of the strap "offends contemporary concepts of decency and human dignity and precepts of civilization."

Even so, physical punishment is not completely prohibited. The only government-run institutions where it is allowed today as a form of discipline are public schools in nearly half the states.

In Florida, a junior-high student named James Ingraham received a severe paddling for walking too slowly off the stage of the school auditorium. A teacher hit James with a paddle twenty times while he was being held down on a table in the principal's office. He suffered bruises that required medical attention and kept him out of school for several days.

James's parents sued the school authorities. They claimed that paddling violates the Eighth Amendment prohibition against cruel and unusual punishments.

The case was decided by the Supreme Court in 1977. In a 5-to-4 decision, the Court ruled in *Ingraham v. Wright* that "moderate" physical punishment, such as spanking or paddling, is acceptable under the Eighth Amendment when it is "reasonable and necessary" for the proper education and discipline of a student. The decision meant that a public school system may permit teachers or other school officials to hit students without violating the Constitution, as long as the punishment is not "excessive." Supervision by the community, said the Court, is a sufficient safeguard against abuses.

Despite that ruling, half the states and a large number of local school districts have passed laws and regulations that forbid school officials from hitting students. And the minority of schools that still permit physical punishment usually have strict rules that limit its use. Critics of the practice say that a school doesn't set a very good example if it can't control students' behavior without hitting them.

In many countries, physical punishment isn't even questioned. An American teenager, eighteen-year-old Michael Fay, became an international celebrity in 1994 when he found himself in trouble with authorities in Singapore, where he was living with his family. Michael was convicted with some other boys of spray-painting graffiti on parked cars. He was sentenced to six painful lashes with a wet rattan cane—a traditional punishment in Singapore.

The case caused headlines throughout the United States. Michael and his father were surprised to learn that a large segment of the American public supported the punishment. Some politicians urged the use of similar punishments in America. After President Bill Clinton interceded, the six lashes were reduced to four, Michael endured his punishment, and then came home. In his hometown of Kettering, Ohio, he probably would have been fined, put on probation, and ordered to pay damages to the car owners.

What does the Eighth Amendment say about the *ultimate* punishment—capital punishment, otherwise known as the death penalty?

In 1890, the Supreme Court ruled that the death penalty is neither cruel nor unusual, as long as it is carried out as swiftly and painlessly as possible. After the ruling, various states imposed the death penalty for a variety of crimes.

Facing press photographers, teenager Michael Fay leaves the Queenstown Prison in Singapore after he was flogged with a wet rattan cane for committing vandalism. His father, George, is directly behind him. *AP/Wide World Photos*

In 1972, the Supreme Court agreed to consider the question again. This time, in a case called *Furman v. Georgia,* the Court ruled that capital punishment, as it was then being administered by the states, violated the Eighth Amendment because of the "arbitrary and capricious" way in which the death penalty was being imposed. In most states, there were no

Some 20,000 people turned out in Owensboro, Kentucky, on August 14, 1936, to witness the last state-sanctioned public execution in America—the hanging of Rainey Bethea, a twenty-two-year-old black man convicted of raping and killing an elderly white woman. Eighteen months after the execution, Kentucky's governor signed a bill outlawing public executions, thus ending the practice in America. *Owensboro Museum of Science and History*

clear guidelines to determine who should or should not be executed. Judges and juries had unlimited discretion to decide if and when to impose a sentence of death. "People live or die, dependent on the whim of one man or of twelve," said Justice William O. Douglas. The result, according to the Court, was that the death sentence was meted out unfairly.

To meet the Supreme Court's objections, thirty-five states passed new death penalty laws. And in 1976, in the case of *Gregg v. Georgia,* the Court said that executions could be resumed. "We now hold," the Court wrote, "that the punishment of death does not invariably violate the Constitution." Once again, the meaning of "cruel and unusual punishments" was to be decided by public opinion or, as the Court put it, by "evolving standards of decency that mark the progress of a maturing society."

By the year 2002, thirty-eight states allowed capital punishment. Depending on the state, executions could be carried out by means of lethal injection, the gas chamber, the electric chair, by hanging, or, in Idaho and Utah, by firing squad. The United States stood almost alone among industrialized democracies in permitting capital punishment, which had been banned by 109 nations worldwide, including Canada, Mexico, and all fifteen countries of the European Union.

Advocates of the death penalty believe that society is justified in taking the life of a cold-blooded killer. And they argue that capital punishment acts as a deterrent—it discourages people from committing murder.

Both arguments are disputed by opponents of the death penalty. Virtually every study ever made, they say, proves that capital punishment has no effect whatever in preventing murder. And they believe that deliberately taking the life of anyone, even a murderer, as a matter of social retribution, is a barbaric act that serves no useful social purpose.

The death penalty has also been challenged on the grounds that it has been imposed in an unfair and discriminatory manner. The poor are likelier than the rich to be executed, and blacks convicted of killing whites are far likelier to be sentenced to death than any other category of defendant.

LEFT:
The electric chair at the Southern Ohio Correctional Facility in Lucasville, Ohio, being dismantled in February 2002. Death by electrocution would no longer be permitted in the state. Three hundred and fifteen inmates were executed in the chair.
AP/Wide World Photos

BELOW:
The lethal injection room at the Mississippi State Penitentiary in Parchman, Mississippi. Witnesses of the executions sit unseen behind the one-way mirrored window.
AP/Wide World Photos

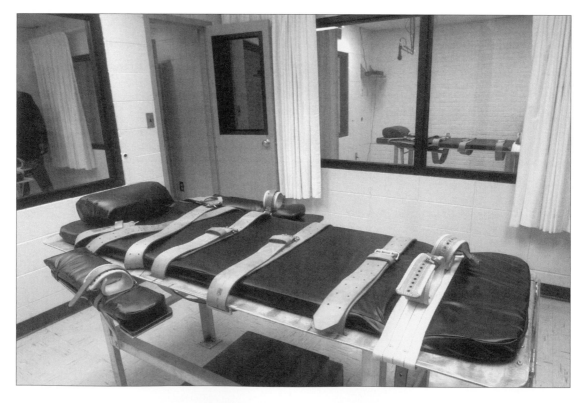

Many prisoners on death row—anywhere from one-tenth to one-third, according to some estimates—are mentally retarded, meaning that they have IQ scores of less than 70. Studies suggest that these prisoners may lack the ability to understand the legal system and participate fully in their own defense. And they are far more likely than others to confess to crimes they did not commit.

In 1989, the Supreme Court refused to declare that executing the retarded should be considered "cruel and unusual punishment." Once again, the Court said that the meaning of "cruel and unusual" must be established by social consensus—by public opinion. The justices held that there wasn't enough of a national consensus to conclude that such executions violated the nation's "evolving standards of decency."

By 2002, however, changing public opinion had prompted eighteen of the thirty-eight states that allowed capital punishment to ban executing the mentally retarded. Other states were considering similar legislation. And the Supreme Court, looking at the question again, made a dramatic turnaround. It reversed its 1989 decision and declared for the first time that executing the retarded does in fact violate the Constitution.

Ruling 6-to-3 in the case of *Atkins v. Virginia*, the Court observed that the tide of public opinion had turned and that a "national consensus" now rejected executions of the retarded as excessive and inappropriate. Daryl R. Atkins, a Virginia man with an IQ of 59, had been convicted of committing a murder and robbery at the age of eighteen. The fifteen nations of the European Union had filed an appeal on Atkins's behalf, as did a group of senior American diplomats. They told the Court that the practice of executing retarded offenders was out of step with much of the world and was a source of friction between the United States and other countries.

Until 2002, the United States had been one of only three nations—the others were Japan and Kyrgyzstan—that permitted the execution of the retarded. For the time being, the United States remained the only western nation to impose death sentences on people younger than eighteen. The Supreme Court ruled in 1989 that the Constitution permits the states to execute convicted murderers who were as young as sixteen when they committed their crimes. Only five other countries were known to execute juvenile criminals: Iran, Yemen, Saudi Arabia, Pakistan, and Nigeria.

In recent years, DNA testing has shown conclusively that many innocent people have been convicted of capital crimes that they did not commit. One man, Ray Krone, spent ten years in an Arizona prison for sexual assault and murder, including time on death row, before being freed in 2002 after a DNA test exonerated him and cast suspicion on another prisoner. According to the Death Penalty Information Center, Krone's release marked an alarming milestone: he was the one hundredth *innocent* person nearly put to death in the United States since 1973. "For ten years," he told a reporter, "I felt less than human."

Another innocent death-row inmate, Anthony Porter, almost did not make it home. Convicted of murder in Illinois, he came within fifty hours

The death sentence of Daryl Atkins, convicted of carjacking and killing an airman in Virginia, was struck down by the Supreme Court in June 2002. Overturning an earlier decision, the Court barred the death penalty for retarded defendants.
AP/Wide World Photos

A jubilant Ray Krone (at left) and his attorney, Alan Simpson, talk with reporters in Mesa, Arizona, after a judge dismissed murder charges against Krone, April 29, 2002. Krone spent ten years in prison for the murder of Kim Ancona until DNA tests proved his innocence. *AP/Wide World Photos*

of being lethally injected before young journalism students at Northwestern University dug up evidence that cleared Porter and led to the arrest of another man.

After twelve other death-row prisoners in Illinois were found to be innocent, Governor George Ryan shocked the nation by ordering a temporary halt to all executions in his state. Ryan appointed a bipartisan commission to study the issue. The commission's report, issued early in 2002, recommended a sweeping overhaul of the state's capital punishment system, with a majority of the members concluding that the death penalty should be abolished. "No system, given human nature and frailties, could ever be devised or constructed that would work perfectly and guarantee absolutely that no innocent person is ever again sentenced to death," the commission said.

Governor Ryan must have given a great deal of thought to the commission's findings. In January 2003, two days before his term in office expired, he made a dramatic announcement that emptied his state's death row. Ryan commuted the death sentences of 167 Illinois prisoners—four of them women—to life in prison, saying that he was "haunted by the demon of error" in criminal prosecutions. He also pardoned four other death-row inmates outright and set them free. The commission had found that their confessions were obtained by police brutality and that prosecutors had suppressed exonerating evidence.

THE NINTH AMENDMENT

The enumeration in the Constitution, of certain rights, shall not be construed to deny or disparage others retained by the people.

11. The Mysterious Ninth

"May we not in the progress of things, discover some great and important [right], which we don't now think of?"—Supreme Court of the Commonwealth of Virginia

What about all those other human rights, the ones that haven't been mentioned so far?

That's what people were asking back in 1789, when the First Congress was debating whether or not to adopt the Bill of Rights. Opponents argued that no bill of rights could ever be comprehensive enough. They feared that if a list of specific rights were added to the Constitution, then other equally fundamental rights that weren't listed would not be protected. "Bills of rights . . . are not only unnecessary in the proposed constitution," wrote Alexander Hamilton, "but would even be dangerous."

James Madison took note of Hamilton's argument. He recognized that no single document could include all the rights of the American people, but he felt that the problem was easily remedied. In addition to the specific rights listed in the first eight amendments, he proposed the Ninth:

> The enumeration in the Constitution, of certain rights, shall not be construed to deny or disparage others retained by the people.

The purpose of the Ninth was to safeguard those rights belonging to the people that weren't named in the first eight amendments. What exactly are those rights? Since the amendment refers to unenumerated, or unlisted, rights without naming them, we can only guess what the authors of the Bill of Rights had in mind.

Alexander Hamilton argued that a bill of rights was not only unnecessary but dangerous, since it could never be comprehensive enough to protect all fundamental rights.
The National Archives

Along with those rights recognized at the time, they might have wanted to provide for new rights that would be revealed or claimed by future generations. "May we not in the progress of things, discover some great and important [right], which we don't now think of?" asked the chief justice of Virginia's highest court.

For nearly two centuries, the Ninth Amendment remained quietly on the sidelines, an unexplored corner of the Bill of Rights. One member of the Supreme Court, Robert H. Jackson, remarked in a speech that the rights secured by the Ninth Amendment were "still a mystery."

But in 1965, the Ninth stepped boldly into the spotlight. For the first time, the Supreme Court cited the amendment as a reason for declaring a state law unconstitutional.

That landmark case, *Griswold v. Connecticut,* concerned a Connecticut law dating back to 1879 that made it a crime to use any kind of birth control device, or contraceptive, even when prescribed by a doctor treating a married couple. Estelle Griswold was director of a medical clinic in New Haven, Connecticut, sponsored by Planned Parenthood, a national organization dedicated to family planning. Dr. C. Lee Buxton was a professor at Yale University and the clinic's medical director. In 1961, they were both arrested and charged with breaking the Connecticut law by providing birth control information to married couples. They were convicted in a state court and fined $100 each.

Griswold and Buxton were deliberately testing the Connecticut law. They appealed, and their case reached the Supreme Court four years later. In a 7-to-2 decision, the Court relied heavily on the Ninth Amendment to

Dr. C. Lee Buxton and Mrs. Estelle T. Griswold hold Planned Parenthood Awards. They were at the center of a landmark case in which the Supreme Court declared, for the first time, that the Constitution protects a personal right to privacy.
Corbis / Bettmann

strike down the Connecticut law, saying that the "right to privacy" had an important bearing on the case. The justices reasoned that any act outlawing birth control could be policed only by invading a married couple's privacy or, as the Court put it, "the sacred precincts of marital bedrooms," and that the right to privacy is protected by the Ninth Amendment, and by other amendments as well.

The word *privacy* never appears in the Constitution. Justice William O. Douglas pointed out that the Supreme Court has long protected many rights that aren't specifically mentioned in the Constitution but are derived from specific provisions of that document. For example, the right to associate with whomever one pleases isn't mentioned anywhere in the Constitution, yet the Court has interpreted the First Amendment as protecting the right of free association.

Douglas argued that around every constitutional provision there exist "buffer zones" that help give those provisions "life and substance." While

Justice William O. Douglas served longer on the Supreme Court (1939 to 1975) and wrote more opinions and more dissents than any justice before or since, including the Court's 1965 privacy decision, *Griswold v. Connecticut*.
The Library of Congress

the right to privacy isn't mentioned specifically, he argued, several provisions of the Bill of Rights create buffer zones of privacy. According to the Third Amendment, soldiers can't invade the privacy of your home. The Fourth Amendment declares that you and your possessions can't be searched without good reason. The Fifth allows a person accused of a crime to remain silent, creating a personal zone of privacy which the government may not force him to surrender. The overall scheme of the Bill of Rights, said Justice Douglas, affirms a fundamental right to privacy for the American people—the right to be left alone.

Critics of the *Griswold* decision accused the Court of treating the Ninth Amendment as a bottomless well in which new rights can be discovered, and of inventing new rights. Supporters of the decision argued that the Ninth should be seen as a guide to interpreting the Constitution, just as the Court interprets equally difficult questions, such as which searches are "reasonable" under the Fourth Amendment, and which punishments "cruel and unusual" under the Eighth. The purpose of the Ninth, they say, is to enumerate new rights as times change, keeping the Bill of Rights a living document that speaks anew to each generation.

Pulled out of the shadows by the *Griswold* case, the Ninth Amendment became a lightning rod of controversy. It was cited in scores of state and federal cases involving not only a right to privacy but an astonishing variety of other individual rights. Schoolboys seeking relief from regulations governing the length of their hair, convicts seeking to avoid imprisonment in the maximum security section of a penitentiary, citizens claiming a right to pure water and unpolluted air—all went to court claiming Ninth Amendment rights. Few of these cases were resolved by the Supreme Court, leaving plenty of room for argument about exactly which rights are "retained by the people" under the Ninth.

The most controversial Ninth Amendment ruling by far concerned the legality of medical abortion—a procedure intended to terminate a pregnancy. In James Madison's day, abortion was legal, if unsafe. The movement to ban abortion began in the mid-1800s; it was motivated by a concern for the safety of women undergoing abortions performed by untrained persons under unsterile conditions, and by mounting moral and religious objections. In 1869, the Catholic Church prohibited abortions under any circumstances. And in both England and the United States, strict antiabortion laws were passed.

In 1970, in a momentous case called *Roe v. Wade*, a federal court in Texas struck down a state law prohibiting abortions unless they were necessary to save the mother's life. The suit had been brought by Jane Roe (a fictitious name to shield her privacy), who challenged the constitutionality of

Norma McCorvey was the anonymous plaintiff Jane Roe of the controversial 1973 abortion case, *Roe v. Wade.* She is shown here celebrating Louisiana Governor Buddy Roemer's veto of a strong antiabortion bill, July 27, 1990. *AP/Wide World Photos*

Activists from both sides of the abortion issue face off outside
the Supreme Court as they wait for a decision to be handed down in 1989.
The pro-life demonstrators at left include a Catholic priest and a protester
holding a poster of a fetus. At right, pro-choice demonstrators hold signs urging
the Court to "Keep Abortion Legal." *Corbis / Bettmann*

the Texas law. She claimed that the law interfered with her personal right
to control her own body and that she had a constitutional right to decide
this matter for herself.

"We agree," wrote the three judges of the Texas court. The state's abortion laws, they said, "must be declared unconstitutional because they
deprive single women and married couples of their right, secured by the
Ninth Amendment, to choose whether to have children."

In 1973, the Supreme Court, by a vote of 7-to-2, upheld the lower court
decision, ruling that a state may not prohibit abortions during the first six

months of pregnancy, and overturning abortion laws throughout the nation. The Court cited a constitutional "right to privacy" based on "the Ninth Amendment's reservation of rights to the people" and on "the Fourteenth Amendment's concept of personal liberty and restrictions upon state action."

Following the *Roe* decision, abortion became an intensely divisive and emotional public issue. Opponents of the decision—members of the "pro-life" movement, as it is called—emphasized the right to life of the unborn and called for a constitutional amendment to make abortion illegal again. They believe that abortion is immoral. They argue that human life begins at conception and that abortion at any stage of pregnancy is murder.

Members of the "pro-choice" movement emphasized each woman's right to make reproductive decisions for herself. They point out that for many women, legal abortion is a matter of life or death. And they reject the claim that abortion is murder, noting that medical professionals and religious leaders alike do not agree on the question of when life begins—whether at conception, at birth, or at some point in between. The insistence that an unborn embryo or fetus is a person, they say, violates freedom of religion by imposing one religious belief on everyone.

When a challenge to the *Roe* decision came before the Supreme Court in 1989, hundreds of thousands of people from both sides demonstrated and counterdemonstrated in the streets of Washington, D.C., attempting to influence both public and judicial opinion. In that case, *Webster v. Reproductive Health Services,* and in other cases since, the Court reaffirmed the right to an abortion but encouraged the states to pass laws restricting the practice.

And so the Ninth Amendment, with its promise of unenumerated individual rights, remains a passionately disputed provision of the Bill of Rights. The courts continue to discover rights not specifically listed in the Constitution, only to meet howls of protest from those who disagree.

"As long as we continue to believe that government is instituted for the sake of securing the rights of the people," writes constitutional scholar Leonard W. Levy, "the Ninth Amendment should have the vitality intended for it."

THE TENTH AMENDMENT

*The powers not delegated to the United States
by the Constitution, nor prohibited by it to the States,
are reserved to the States respectively, or to the people.*

12. The Battle over States' Rights

"The powers delegated . . . to the Federal Government are few and defined. Those which are to remain in the State Governments are numerous and indefinite."
—*James Madison*

In 1916, it seemed that the crusade against child labor in America was going to pay off at long last. Across the country, children who should have been in school or at play were hard at work in factories, mines, fields, and mills. Laborers as young as three years old often held jobs, and many youngsters worked twelve hours or more a day, six days a week, for pitiful wages under unhealthy and dangerous conditions.

Thanks to a persistent campaign by the National Child Labor Committee, Congress had finally passed a Child Labor Law that would apply equally to all American children. While the law made only modest reforms, it was a beginning. It prohibited the transportation across state lines of goods made by businesses that employed children under fourteen, or children between fourteen and sixteen who worked more than eight hours a day, more than six days a week, or on factory night shifts.

But the nation's first Child Labor Law was challenged in the courts and never took effect. In 1918, the Supreme Court ruled that the law was unconstitutional, because it trespassed on states' rights. The landmark decision, *Hammer v. Dagenhart,* cited the powers "reserved to the States" by the Tenth Amendment. The Court agreed that Congress had the power to regulate interstate commerce—trade among the various states. But only the

Breaker boys at a Pennsylvania coal mine, c. 1911. *The Library of Congress*

individual states themselves could regulate working conditions *within* their own boundaries. That meant that child labor laws, if any, had to be passed by each state on its own.

And that's where matters stood until 1938, when Congress made another attempt to regulate child labor across the entire nation. The Fair Labor Standards Act set minimum wage standards for all workers in interstate commerce and placed limitations on child labor. The employment of children under sixteen was prohibited in mining and manufacturing.

This time, the Supreme Court did an about-face and interpreted the Constitution differently. In *United States v. Darby,* 1941, the Court overruled its earlier decision concerning child labor and states' rights. The justices now declared that the Tenth Amendment does *not* prevent the federal government from regulating working conditions within the states.

Those clashing decisions reflect a debate over states' rights that has been going on ever since the nation's founding. At the Constitutional Convention in 1787, the delegates could not agree on how power should be divided between the states and the national government. Sovereign states accustomed to running their own affairs were reluctant to surrender any of their powers to a strong central government.

The solution was to create a *federal* system of government. The states recognized the authority of the national government while retaining certain powers of their own. The Tenth Amendment was written to guarantee that

The powers not delegated to the United States by the Constitution . . . are reserved to the States respectively, or to the people.

The question is: what exactly are those "reserved" powers?

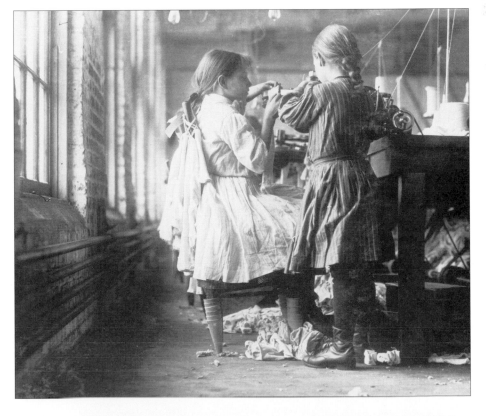

A raveler and a looper in a hosiery mill, Loudon, Tennessee, 1910.
The Library of Congress

Article I of the Constitution lists the powers granted to the national government: among them, the power to raise an army, declare war, conduct foreign policy, coin money, manage trade with other countries, and regulate commerce among the various states. And it lists those powers *prohibited* to the individual states: the states are forbidden to enter into treaties, impose import or export taxes, or keep troops without the consent of Congress. But the Constitution doesn't list the powers "reserved to the States."

James Madison said that "the powers delegated by the proposed Constitution to the Federal Government are few and defined. Those which are to remain in the State Governments are numerous and indefinite. . . . They will extend to all the objects, which, in the ordinary course of affairs, concern the lives, liberties, and prosperities of the people."

The Constitution doesn't spell out what the states may do, but it does say that no state or local law can be in conflict with the Constitution or with national laws. It is generally agreed that the major powers reserved to the states are to tax, spend, and regulate commerce within the state, to exercise police powers, and to govern such matters as marriage, divorce, and the licensing of automobile drivers and others.

Other governmental powers are shared by the national and state governments. Both are concerned with education, public health, criminal justice, and the welfare system. Beyond that, the courts have found it difficult to define all the powers reserved to the states. And when state and federal laws collide, then the Tenth Amendment becomes a legal battleground.

The balance of power between the states and the national government has been debated by every generation of Americans, by those who feel that the federal government is too big and has too much power, and those who believe that we must look to Congress and the Supreme Court to preserve basic constitutional liberties. At times, the states have acted first and done more to protect individual rights. Early in the twentieth century, before Congress passed the first national labor laws, some states enacted laws of their own to improve the terrible working conditions of the time, only to have those laws struck down by the United States Supreme Court.

At other times, the term *states' rights* has been a segregationist battle cry of those who would deprive minorities of the civil rights guaranteed by the Constitution. During the 1960s, the federal government, supported by the Supreme Court, took the lead in passing civil rights legislation and in ordering the desegregation of the nation's schools, against strong state resistance.

The Tenth Amendment is often seen as a companion to the Ninth. Both say that there are rights and powers that aren't spelled out in state or federal constitutions—rights and powers that belong to the people and cannot

Among the powers reserved to the states are laws governing marriage and divorce. This New York couple said their wedding vows on the Cyclone roller-coaster at Coney Island, August 25, 1994. *AP/Wide World Photos*

During the early 1960s, "states' rights" was a segregationist battle cry. On June 12, 1963, Alabama Governor George Wallace blocked the entrance to the University of Alabama, refusing Nicholas Katzenbach of the Justice Department permission to enter the building and enroll two black students. *Corbis/Bettmann*

be infringed by any government. And while both amendments have proven hard to interpret, both make it emphatically clear that the powers of the government are limited.

The Constitution of the United States begins with the words *We, the people.* So it seems fitting that the tenth and last amendment of the Bill of Rights ends with the words *the people,* whom the framers of the Constitution recognized as the source and the justification of all governmental power.

13. Madison's Most Valuable Amendment

"The demand for equal rights became contagious."   Ira Glasser

In 1789, when the United States Congress met for the first time, James Madison proposed the constitutional amendments that would become known as the Bill of Rights. Most of his proposals were approved by Congress, but the one amendment he had singled out as especially important was rejected when it failed to get the necessary two-thirds vote.

The debate in Congress focused on the need for a *national* bill of rights, to limit the powers of the national government. Madison argued that the *state* governments also posed a threat to individual liberties. While the states had their own constitutions, and in some cases, their own bills of rights, Madison believed that additional protections were needed. So he suggested an amendment that read: "No State shall violate the equal rights of conscience, or the freedom of the press, or the trial by jury in criminal cases."

This, in Madison's opinion, was "the most valuable amendment on the list." But his fellow congressmen didn't agree. They decided that the amendment was unnecessary, and it was dropped from the list when Congress voted on the Bill of Rights.

As it turned out, Madison's fears about the states were justified. In the years that followed, most abuses of individual rights were committed by state and local governments. Because Congress had killed Madison's "most valuable amendment," the Supreme Court ruled in 1833 that the Bill of Rights applied only to the national government, not to the states. For example, the First Amendment says, "*Congress* shall make no law . . ."

A family of several generations of slaves on a South Carolina plantation, 1862. The Thirteenth Amendment, ratified in 1865, abolished "slavery and involuntary servitude" in the United States. *The Library of Congress*

The states remained free to violate individual rights as they saw fit, and often they did. States could restrict freedom of religion, censor speech, ban books and newspapers, abolish trial by jury, and imprison people for their political beliefs.

Some Southern states passed laws making it a crime to argue against slavery, to criticize a master's property rights over his slaves, or to send anti-slavery publications through the mail. "Liberty of speech [and] freedom of the press . . . had disappeared in the slave states," said a member of Congress in 1864. The Civil War had to be fought between 1861 and 1865—the bloodiest war in America's history—before Congress passed additional constitutional amendments limiting the power of the states to take away the civil rights of their citizens.

Three constitutional amendments emerged from the Civil War. The Thirteenth Amendment (1865) abolished "slavery and involuntary servitude." The Fifteenth (1870) guaranteed that the right to vote cannot be denied because of race, color, or having previously been a slave.

The Fourteenth Amendment (1868) is the most complex and far-reaching of the three. It defines United States citizenship, places national citizenship above state citizenship, and guarantees every person "equal protection of the laws."

Section 1 of the Fourteenth Amendment declares:

All persons born or naturalized in the United States, and subject to the jurisdiction thereof, are citizens of the United States and of the State wherein they reside. No State shall make or enforce any law which shall abridge the privileges or immunities of citizens of the United States; nor shall any State deprive any person of life, liberty, or property, without due process of law; nor deny to any person within its jurisdiction the equal protection of the laws.

With the passage of these amendments, the federal Constitution, for the first time, began to protect individuals against the states. The Fourteenth, in particular, made possible the extension of civil and political liberties to *all* citizens, regardless of sex, race, religion, national origin, status, or wealth. And yet this possibility, this promise, was not fulfilled at first. It

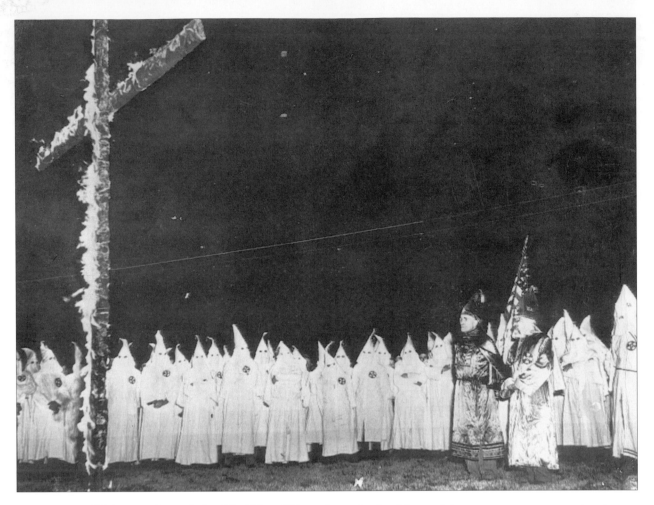

This meeting of the Ku Klux Klan, America's oldest white supremacy organization, took place at Wrightsville, Georgia, in 1948. Hidden behind their hoods, Klansmen enforced racial segregation and terrorized their enemies, black and white alike, by means of intimidation, violence, and lynchings. *The National Archives*

would be a long time before the amendment's lofty principles came to be realized in practice as meaningful individual rights for all citizens.

For almost a century, African-American citizens were denied the equal protection of the laws promised by the Fourteenth Amendment. Written and unwritten laws, called Jim Crow laws, enforced by intimidation, violence, and lynchings, continued to foster racial segregation, prevent blacks from voting, and exclude them from much of social and political life. It wasn't until well into the twentieth century that the struggles of black

Americans to gain equal rights resulted in court rulings that finally unleashed the power of the slumbering Fourteenth Amendment and applied the Bill of Rights to state and local governments.

One of the most important cases ever decided by the Supreme Court was called *Brown v. Board of Education*. Linda Brown was a seven-year-old who attended an all-black school about a mile from her home in Topeka, Kansas. Every morning, she made her way through railroad switching yards and past rows of warehouses on streets without sidewalks before boarding the bus that took her the rest of the way to school.

In 1950, Linda's father, Oliver Brown, took his daughter by the hand and tried to register her at a school for white children just seven blocks from their home. When the school authorities refused to enroll Linda, her father filed suit with the help of lawyers from the NAACP—the National Association for the Advancement of Colored People—challenging Topeka's segregated school system. The *Brown* case was eventually joined by four other school segregation cases filed in Virginia, the District of Columbia, Delaware, and South Carolina.

In an unheated classroom at a segregated South Carolina school, African-American students sit three to a seat measuring 36 inches wide, November 15, 1934.
The Library of Congress

Protesters in St. Louis demand an end to school segregation. *The National Archives*

On May 17, 1954, in a momentous decision that would affect race relations across America, the Supreme Court unanimously struck down state-enforced school segregation. The Court declared that racial segregation in public schools denied black children equal protection of the laws as guaranteed by the Fourteenth Amendment. "To separate [children] from others of similar age and qualifications solely because of their race," wrote Chief Justice Earl Warren, "generates a feeling of inferiority as to their status in the community that may affect their hearts and minds in a way unlikely ever to be undone."

By desegregating public schools and colleges, *Brown* signaled the end of a Jim Crow rule that had dominated the country since the Civil War. From that time on, the Fourteenth Amendment was recognized as a key legal basis for the expanding civil rights movement. Despite hostility and resistance, some of it violent, the movement for equality spread to all sections of society.

"The demand for equal rights became contagious," writes Ira Glasser, executive director of the American Civil Liberties Union. "Women seeking an end to discrimination based on sex were the first, but they were far from the last. . . . Equal rights became a rallying cry for groups never before thought to be protected by the Bill of Rights: Asians, Hispanics, American Indians, gay people, children in school and foster care, people with disabilities, soldiers, inmates of mental institutions, prisoners, aliens, and those too poor to protect their rights in a wide variety of legal proceedings. All began to see the Bill of Rights as a weapon they might use, as black citizens had, to gain rights they had long been denied."

As chief lawyer for the NAACP, Thurgood Marshall challenged racial discrimination in many areas of American life. His most famous case was *Brown v. Board of Education*, which in 1954 struck down state-enforced school segregation. In 1967 he became the first African-American member of the Supreme Court, where he served until 1991. *The National Archives*

More than 200,000 black and white Americans from all over the country fill the area around the Washington Monument Reflecting Pool during ceremonies at the Civil Rights March on Washington, D.C., August 28, 1963. The march was organized to support proposed civil rights legislation and end segregation. *AP/Wide World Photos*

The courts, meanwhile, were moving gradually in the direction of saying that the Bill of Rights and the federal Constitution apply to everyone in all situations—which means that the states, as well as the national government, must observe and protect those rights. For this reason, the Fourteenth is usually considered the most important amendment after the original ten and, with the Thirteenth and Fifteenth, is an essential part of the Bill of Rights.

14. The Right to Differ

"Freedom to differ is not limited to things that do not matter much."
—*Justice Robert H. Jackson*

When the Supreme Court ruled that schoolchildren can't be required to salute the American flag and recite the Pledge of Allegiance if it offends their religious beliefs, the justices were protecting the rights of those children and of every other American.

The decision was handed down on Flag Day in 1943, at a time when young Americans were fighting and dying for that flag around the planet. The children concerned were Jehovah's Witnesses, a small religious sect, and in the minds of many, an obscure one. And yet the American people, far from denouncing the Supreme Court decision, recognized it as an eloquent statement of what the country was fighting for.

The state law that required flag salutes and pledges of allegiance in the schools of West Virginia was declared unconstitutional because it violated both the freedom of religion clause and the free speech clause of the First Amendment. The salute and pledge are a form of speech, said the Court. And the government cannot compel citizens to express beliefs without violating freedom of speech. That freedom has to be respected, whether objections to saluting the flag are religiously based or not.

The Court's majority opinion, written by Justice Robert H. Jackson, became one of the great statements in American constitutional law and history. "Freedom to differ," he wrote, "is not limited to things that do not matter much. That would be a mere shadow of freedom. The test of [free-

A panoramic view of the Civil Rights March on Washington, D. C., taken from atop the Lincoln Memorial. *The National Archives*

dom's] substance is the right to differ as to things that touch the heart of the existing order."

The United States is a democracy, a nation in which most political decisions are made by majority rule. We may like to think that democracy and liberty go hand in hand, but that is not necessarily so. Even in a democracy, the rule of the majority must be limited so that individual liberty can be preserved. The majority can't be allowed to rule everything.

The original American citizens recognized that people have rights that no majority should be able to take away. A bill of rights, wrote James Winthrop of Massachusetts, "serves to secure the minority against the usurpations and tyranny of the majority."

After two hundred years, we are still striving to realize the ideals expressed in the Bill of Rights, and to extend equal rights under the law to all Americans. When the United States has been faced with crisis or war, we have sometimes yielded to fear and allowed our constitutional liberties to be threatened. It is easy to tolerate dissent when we feel safe. Our commitment to freedom under law is put to its hardest test at times of peril and doubt.

The Bill of Rights promises that every person is entitled to have his or her rights respected. We enjoy those rights today because so many ordinary citizens have had the courage to challenge arbitrary government power and raise their voices at injustice.

"Liberty," said Judge Learned Hand, "lies in the hearts of men and women. When it dies there, no constitution, no law, no court can save it."

THE BILL OF RIGHTS

AMENDMENT I

Congress shall make no law respecting an establishment of religion, or prohibiting the free exercise thereof; or abridging the freedom of speech, or of the press; or the right of the people peaceably to assemble, and to petition the Government for a redress of grievances.

AMENDMENT II

A well regulated Militia, being necessary to the security of a free State, the right of the people to keep and bear Arms, shall not be infringed.

AMENDMENT III

No Soldier shall, in time of peace be quartered in any house, without the consent of the Owner, nor in time of war, but in a manner to be prescribed by law.

AMENDMENT IV

The right of the people to be secure in their persons, houses, papers, and effects, against unreasonable searches and seizures, shall not be violated, and no Warrants shall issue, but upon probable cause, supported by Oath or affirmation, and particularly describing the place to be searched, and the persons or things to be seized.

AMENDMENT V

No person shall be held to answer for a capital, or otherwise infamous crime, unless on a presentment or indictment of a Grand Jury, except in cases arising in the land or naval forces, or in the Militia, when in actual service in time of War or public danger; nor shall any person be subject for the same offence to be twice put in jeopardy of life or limb; nor shall be compelled in any criminal case to be a witness against himself, nor be deprived of life, liberty, or property, without due process of law; nor shall private property be taken for public use, without just compensation.

AMENDMENT VI

In all criminal prosecutions, the accused shall enjoy the right to a speedy and public trial, by an impartial jury of the State and district wherein the crime shall have been committed, which district shall have been previously ascertained by law, and to be informed of the nature and cause of the accusation; to be confronted with the witnesses against him; to have compulsory process for obtaining witnesses in his favor, and to have the Assistance of Counsel for his defence.

AMENDMENT VII

In suits at common law, where the value in controversy shall exceed twenty dollars, the right of trial by jury shall be preserved, and no fact tried by a jury, shall be otherwise reexamined in any Court of the United States, than according to the rules of the common law.

AMENDMENT VIII

Excessive bail shall not be required, nor excessive fines imposed, nor cruel and unusual punishments inflicted.

AMENDMENT IX

The enumeration in the Constitution, of certain rights, shall not be construed to deny or disparage others retained by the people.

AMENDMENT X

The powers not delegated to the United States by the Constitution, nor prohibited by it to the States, are reserved to the States respectively, or to the people.

The Bill of Rights, engrossed on a sheet of parchment, is on permanent
display at the National Archives building in Washington, D.C., along with the Constitution and
the Declaration of Independence.

The Library of Congress

NOTES

The notes for this book consist largely of citations to the source of quoted material. Each citation includes the first few words and the last word or phrase of the quotation, and its source. Unless otherwise noted, references are to books cited in the bibliography. Also noted are the sources of certain statistics.

Chapter 2. Why We Have the Bill of Rights

Page

9 "a feeble thread": quoted in Bobrick, p. 488

10 "No constitution . . . public": quoted in Fleming, p. 358

13 "the infernal traffic," "the judgment of heaven": quoted in Fleming, p. 366

13 "not be parties to the Union": quoted in Fleming, p. 366

14 "It would . . . people": quoted in Levy, 1999, p. 33

14 "a few hours": quoted in Levy, 1999, p. 13

14 "I confess . . . them": quoted in Fleming, p. 368

15 "wicked, cruel, and unnatural": quoted in Meltzer, p. 30

16 "A bill . . . refuse": quoted in Levy, 1999, p. 26

Chapter 3. Freedom of Religion

Page

23–24 "I do not . . . commandments": "Pledge Dispute Evokes Bitter Memories," *New York Times*, September 11, 1988

27–28 Church statistics cited in Fleming, p. 24

29 "universal alarm . . . Parliament," "bishops . . . all other churches": quoted in Glasser, p. 72

30 "The right . . . toleration": quoted in "Church and State, Separation of," *The Young Readers Companion to American History*, John A. Garraty, ed. (Boston: Houghton Mifflin, 1994), p. 147

30 "a wall . . . state": quoted in Brant, p. 401

32 "neutral in . . . religion," "genuine choice": "Supreme Court Upholds Voucher System," *New York Times*, June 28, 2002

32 "Whenever we . . . democracy": "The Wrong Ruling on Vouchers" (editorial), *New York Times*, June 28, 2002

34 "to control . . . say": quoted in Glasser, p. 89

35 "punishment for bad conduct": quoted in Alderman & Kennedy, 1991, p. 411

35 "forbids the . . . graudation": quoted in Alderman & Kennedy, 1991, p. 413

35 "attacked, twisted, and warped": quoted in Alderman & Kennedy, 1991, p. 413

36 "The very . . . elections": quoted in Irons, p. 345

36 "in any form": Glasser, p. 82

37 "purely ethical creed": Glasser, p. 82

40 "If there . . . therein": quoted in Irons, p. 345

40 "without the . . . Government": quoted in Levy, 1999, p. 86

Chapter 4. Freedom of Expression

Page

43 "disruptive influence": Cary, Levine, & Price, p. 32

44 "materially and . . . school": quoted in Cary et al., p. 29

44 "It need . . . Constitution": quoted in Nunez & Marx, p. 52

45 "The young . . . today": quoted in Nunez & Marx, p. 55

46 "the germ . . . America": Alderman & Kennedy, 1991, p. 153

49 "falsely shouting . . . panic," "a clear . . . prevent": quoted in Brant, p. 393

50   "assert your rights": quoted in Glasser, p. 126

51   "There is no time . . . liberty": quoted in Irons, p. 283

51–52   "utterly illegal . . . laws": quoted in Irons, p. 283

52   "I think . . . country": quoted in Brant, p. 395

52   "Those who won . . . truth": quoted in Foner, p. 185

53   "safe": quoted in Foner, p. 256

53   "were not charged . . . forcible overthrow of the Government": quoted in Glasser, p. 132

55   "I think . . . in America": quoted in Meltzer, pp. 93–94

57   "under our . . . idea": quoted in Glasser, p. 137

58   "Public expression . . . hearers": quoted in Alderman & Kennedy, 1991, p. 30

59   "You take . . . gone": quoted in Krull, p. 56

60   "an environment . . . students": quoted in Cary et al., p. 54

60   "may not . . . system": quoted in Cary et al., pp. 54–55

62   "First Amendment . . . thought": " 'Virtual' Child Pornography Ban Overturned," *New York Times*, April 17, 2002

Chapter 5. The Right to Bear Arms?

Page

65   "the embarrassing Second Amendment": William Glaberson, "Right to Bear Arms: A Second Look," *New York Times*, June 30, 1999

65   "the murky Second": William Safire, "An Appeal for Repeal," *New York Times*, June 10, 1999

65   "the orphan . . . Rights": William Glaberson, "Right to Bear Arms: A Second Look," *New York Times*, June 30, 1999

65   Gunshot statistics are from "On 8th Anniversary of Brady Law, Gun Deaths Are Down 27 Percent," Brady Campaign press release, November 29, 2001

66 Children's firearms death statistics are from "Kids and Guns in America," Brady Campaign issue brief, January 13, 2002

67–68 "To place . . . desertions": quoted in Bobrick, p. 327

69 "as the instrument . . . peoples": quoted in Bobrick, p. 326

69 "To preserve . . . shooting range," "Fax machines . . . of all": Amar, p. 49

71 "We think . . . unconstitutional": "Ashcroft Supports Broad View of Gun Rights," *New York Times,* May 24, 2001

71 "obvious purpose . . . effectiveness": quoted in "The Second Amendment," Brady Campaign issue brief, January 13, 2002

71 "some reasonable . . . militia": quoted in "An Ominous Reversal on Gun Rights," *New York Times,* May 14, 2002

71 "that its use . . . defense": quoted in "Whose Right to Bear Arms?" (letters), *New York Times,* November 1, 1999

71–72 "The very language . . . firearms": quoted in "The Second Amendment," Brady Campaign issue brief, January 13, 2002

73 "the Second Amendment . . . exceptions": "Court Says Individuals Have a Right to Firearms," *New York Times,* October 17, 2001

73 "there exists . . . somewhat cryptic": *New York Times,* December 6, 2002

74 "almost no right . . . exercise," "The right to bear arms . . . scrutiny": "Well-Regulated Militias, and More," *New York Times,* October 28, 1999

75 "Our current . . . terrorists": "Lawmakers See Terror Risk in Gun Law Loopholes," Reuters, December 19, 2001

76 "The war . . . citizens": "Lawmakers See Terror Risk . . . ," Reuters, December 19, 2001

Chapter 6. The Right to Be Left Alone: Uninvited Guests

Page

80 "It is downright . . . wrong!": quoted in Alderman & Kennedy, 1991, p. 108

82 "This provision . . . peril": quoted in Alderman & Kennedy, 1991, p. 110

Chapter 7. The Right to Be Left Alone: Searches and Seizures
Page

87 "The poorest . . . tenement": quoted in Levy, 1999, p. 151

87 "Thus our houses . . . towns": quoted in Levy, 1999, p. 166

90–91 "the right . . . Amendment": quoted in Alderman & Kennedy, 1991, p. 136

91 "progress of science . . . espionage": quoted in Glasser, p. 174

92 "more sophisticated systems," "leave the homeowner . . . technology," "The Fourth . . . bright": "Justices Say Warrant Is Required in High-Tech Searches of Homes," *New York Times*, June 12, 2001

96 "the freedoms . . . protect": "Stir Over U.S. Eavesdropping," *New York Times*, November 8, 2001

96 "reasonable suspicion": Cary et al., p. 116

98 "School sports . . . bashful": quoted in Nunez & Marx, p. 93

98 "far more reasonable": quoted in Hall, p. 318

Chapter 8. The Right to Remain Silent
Page

103 "I am not . . . examination": quoted in Alderman & Kennedy, 1991, p. 170

103 "though I be . . . horses": quoted in Glasser, p. 160

103 "I was condemned . . . myself": quoted in Alderman & Kennedy, 1991, p. 171

106 "to confess . . . crime": Levy, 1999, p. 198

106 "bloody . . . tyrannous": Brant, p. 113

111 "custodial interrogation . . . intimidation": quoted in Hall, p. 193

111 "system of criminal . . . mouth": quoted in Alderman & Kennedy, 1991, p. 172

112 "will return . . . streets": quoted in Irons, p. 418

112 American Bar Association survey cited by Glasser, p. 164

Chapter 9. The Right to a Fair Trial

Page

116 "The institution . . . government": quoted in Amar, p. 88

117 "without being . . . law": Glasser, p. 159

118 "systematic exclusion," "fair cross-section requirement": quoted in Krull, p. 159

122 "cannot be realized . . . him": quoted in Brant, p. 473

123–24 "Under our . . . court": quoted in Nunez & Marx, p. 129

126 "grave injustice . . . leadership": quoted in Irons, p. 361

127 "Ancestry is not a crime": quoted in Irons, p. 361

127 "Secret arrests . . . society": "After September 11, a Legal Battle on the Limits of Civil Liberty," *New York Times*, August 4, 2002

128 "Those who . . . safety": quoted in Bob Herbert, "Isn't Democracy Worth It?" *New York Times*, June 17, 2002

Chapter 10. Cruel and Unusual Punishment

Page

131 "hanged up . . . souls": quoted in Glasser, p. 115

131 "barbarous . . . unjust": quoted in Levy, 1999, p. 237

134 "for bodilie . . . cruell": quoted in Levy, 1999, p. 237

135 "It is sometimes . . . cruel?" quoted in Brant, p. 71

135 "is not . . . practice": quoted in Meltzer, p. 147

135 "offends . . . civilization": quoted in Cary et al., p. 107

136 "moderate": Cary et al., p. 107

136 "reasonable and necessary": Nunez & Marx, p. 139

136 "excessive": Cary, et al., p. 109

138 "arbitrary and capricious": quoted in Alderman & Kennedy, 1991, p. 300

139 "People live . . . twelve": quoted in Alderman & Kennedy, 1991, p. 299

139 "We now hold . . . Constitution": quoted in Alderman & Kennedy, 1991, p. 300

139 "evolving standards of . . . society": "Top Court Hears Argument on Execution of Retarded," *New York Times*, February 21, 2002

139 Capital punishment banned by 109 nations: "An Execution in Texas Strains Ties With Mexico and Others," *New York Times*, August 16, 2002

141 "national consensus": "Citing 'National Consensus,' Justices Bar Death Penalty for Retarded Defendants," *New York Times*, June 21, 2002

142 one hundredth *innocent* person: "Death Is Different" (editorial), *New York Times*, April 10, 2002

142 "For ten . . . human": Interview on National Public Radio, April 13, 2002

143 "No system . . . death": "Panel in Illinois Seeks to Reform Death Sentence," *New York Times*, April 15, 2002

144 "haunted by . . . error": *Washington Spectator*, February 1, 2003

Chapter 11. The Mysterious Ninth

Page

147 "Bills of rights . . . dangerous": quoted in Alderman & Kennedy, 1991, p. 319

148 "May we not . . . think of?": quoted in Levy, 1999, p. 255

148 "still a mystery": quoted in Levy, 1999, p. 241

150 "the sacred . . . bedrooms": quoted in Levy, 1999, p. 242

150 "life and substance": quoted in Alderman & Kennedy, 1991, p. 318

153 "We agree . . . children": quoted in Irons, p. 434

154 "right to privacy . . . action": quoted in Alderman & Kennedy, 1991, p. 322

154 "As long . . . for it": Levy, 1999, p. 260

Chapter 12. The Battle over States' Rights

Page

160 "The powers . . . people": quoted in Alderman & Kennedy, 1991, p. 328

Chapter 13. Madison's Most Valuable Amendment

Page

163 "No State . . . cases": quoted in Levy, 1999, p. 283

163 "the most . . . list": quoted in Glasser, p. 44

165 "Liberty of speech . . . states": quoted in Glasser, p. 123

168 "To separate . . . undone": quoted in Brant, p. 371

169 "The demand . . . denied": Glasser, p. 217

Chapter 14. The Right to Differ

Page

171–72 "Freedom to differ . . . order": quoted in Alderman & Kennedy, 1991, p. 338

173 "serves to secure . . . majority": quoted in Glasser, p. 41

173 "Liberty lies . . . save it": quoted in Glasser, p. 13

INDEX OF SUPREME COURT CASES

Supreme Court decisions are recorded in a multivolume set of books called *United States Reports* (abbreviated *U.S.*). The names of the parties involved in the case come first, followed by the volume number, the page on which the case begins, and finally the date of the decision. For example, *370 U.S. 421 (1962)* indicates that the case appears in volume 370 of *United States Reports* on page 421 and was decided by the Supreme Court in 1962. Recent cases that were not yet included in bound volumes when this book went to press are identified by their Supreme Court docket number.

The librarian at a law school or a library that has law books can help locate any of the decisions cited in this book. Decisions are also available on-line at the following websites:

www.supremecourtus.gov/
www.supct.law.cornell.edu/supct/
www.fedworld.gov/supcourt/

Chapter 3. Freedom of Religion

Chapter 4. Freedom of Expression

Chapter 5. The Right to Bear Arms?

Page

Chapter 7. The Right to Be Left Alone: Searches and Seizures

Page

Chapter 8. The Right to Remain Silent

Page

Chapter 9. The Right to a Fair Trial

Page

Chapter 10. Cruel and Unusual Punishment

Chapter 11. The Mysterious Ninth

Chapter 12. The Battle over States' Rights

Chapter 13. Madison's Most Valuable Amendment

SELECTED BIBLIOGRAPHY

A visionary document, the Bill of Rights remains as vital and as controversial today as it was at the nation's founding. It is the subject of a vast literature dealing with the origins of our civil liberties, with analyses and interpretations of the various amendments and of landmark Supreme Court decisions, and with the continuous and ongoing struggle to implement and secure the written guarantees added to the Constitution in 1791.

I found the following books especially helpful:

Ira Glasser's *Visions of Liberty: The Bill of Rights for All Americans* (New York: Little, Brown, 1991), an eloquent work by the former director of the American Civil Liberties Union, surveys the historical background of the Bill of Rights and focuses on freedom of conscience and expression, and on issues of fundamental fairness, racial equality, and minority rights. Ellen Alderman and Caroline Kennedy's *In Our Defense: The Bill of Rights in Action* (New York: William Morrow, 1991) discusses the legal significance of each amendment in terms of the stories of ordinary Americans whose lives have been deeply affected by civil rights issues. Peter Irons's *A People's History of the Supreme Court* (New York: Viking Penguin, 1999) also offers accounts of citizens who have brought cases before the Supreme Court, along with revealing sketches of the justices who decide what the Constitution means. Irving Brant's *The Bill of Rights: Its Origin and Meaning* (New York: New American Library, 1967) remains an indispensible scholarly study of the Constitution from its roots in English common law to the landmark Supreme Court decisions of the 1960s.

Two recent works of constitutional scholarship and interpretation offer valuable insights. Leonard W. Levy's *Origins of the Bill of Rights* (New Haven: Yale University Press, 1999), a discussion of the historical background of each amendment, is by a noted scholar and author of thirty-five other books, including *Origins of the Fifth Amendment* (New York: Macmillan, 1986 reprint), for which he received the Pulitzer Prize in 1969. Akhil Reed Amar's *The Bill of Rights: Creation and Reconstruction* (New Haven: Yale University Press, 1998) is an analysis by a leading legal scholar of the political values that have informed and influenced the Bill of Rights.

The Oxford Guide to United States Supreme Court Decisions, edited by Kermit L. Hall (New York: Oxford University Press, 1999), includes brief commentaries on 440 of the Court's most important cases; it is an updated paperback version of the authoritative *Oxford Companion to the Supreme Court of the United States,* edited by Hall and published in 1991.

Roots of the Bill of Rights: An Illustrated Documentary History, edited by Bernard Schwartz (New York: Chelsea House, 1981), offers a massive compilation of documents dealing with the Bill of Rights from its English and colonial sources to its final ratification by the states; this work is often cited in Supreme Court decisions.

Two lively accounts of events and personalities during America's revolutionary period are Benson Bobrick's *Angel in the Whirlwind: The Triumph of the American Revolution* (New York: Simon & Schuster, 1997) and Thomas Fleming's *Liberty: The American Revolution* (New York: Viking, 1997). Eric Foner's *The Story of American Freedom* (New York: W. W. Norton, 1998) is an illuminating history of America from the Revolution to our own time, focused on the continuing struggle to define and achieve freedom. For events in England leading up to the American Revolution, I consulted two popular works: G. M. Trevelyan's *A Shortened History of England* (New York: Penguin Books, 1987), an abridged edition of Trevelyan's classic study, *A History of England,* and F. E. Halliday's *England: A Concise History* (New York: Thames & Hudson, 1989).

Noteworthy works that address specific constitutional issues include William Lee Miller's *The First Liberty: Religion and the American Republic* (New York: Alfred A. Knopf, 1986); Rodney A. Smolla's *Free Speech in an Open Society* (New York: Alfred A. Knopf, 1992); Donna A. Demac's *Liberty Denied: The Current Rise of Censorship in*

America (New York: Pen American Center, 1988); Osha Gray Davidson's *Under Fire: The NRA and the Battle for Gun Control* (Iowa City, Iowa: University of Iowa Press, 1998); Robert Jay Lifton and Greg Mitchell's *Who Owns Death? Capital Punishment, the American Conscience, and the End of Executions* (New York: HarperCollins, 2000); and Ellen Alderman and Caroline Kennedy's *The Right to Privacy* (New York: Alfred A. Knopf, 1995).

The Rights of Students by Eve Cary, Alan H. Levine, and Janet Price (New York: Puffin Books, 1997) is one of the American Civil Liberties Union's Handbooks for Young Americans. *The American Heritage History of the Bill of Rights* by Philip A. Klinker et al. (Englewood Cliffs, New Jersey: Silver Burdett, 1991) devotes separate volumes to each amendment in a ten-volume series.

Other recommended titles for young readers include Leah Farish's *The First Amendment: Freedom of Speech, Religion, and the Press* (Springfield, New Jersey: Enslow, 1998); Kathleen Krull's *A Kid's Guide to America's Bill of Rights: Curfews, Censorship, and the 100-Pound Giant* (New York: Avon Books, 1999); Edmund Lindop's *The Bill of Rights and Landmark Cases* (New York: Franklin Watts, 1989); Milton Meltzer's *The Bill of Rights: How We Got It and What It Means* (New York: Thomas Y. Crowell, 1990); Sandra Nunez and Trish Marx's *And Justice for All: The Legal Rights of Young People* (Brookfield, Connecticut: The Millbrook Press, 1997); Doreen Rappaport's *Tinker v. Des Moines: Student Rights on Trial* (New York: HarperCollins, 1993); Victoria Sherrow's *Freedom of Worship* (Brookfield, Connecticut: The Millbrook Press, 1997); and Richard Steins's *Censorship: How Does It Conflict With Freedom?* (New York: Twenty-First Century Books, 1997).

Among the numerous websites devoted to constitutional issues and civil liberties are:

American Civil Liberties Union at www.aclu.org

American Library Association Office for Intellectual Freedom at
    www.ala.org/oif.html/

Americans United for Separation of Church and State at www.au.org

The Brady Campaign to Prevent Gun Violence at
    www.handguncontrol.org/
Freedom Forum (speech and press freedom) at
    www.freedomforum.org/
National Coalition to Abolish the Death Penalty at www.ncadp.org/
National Rifle Association at www.nra.org/
Religious Freedom website at www.religious-freedom.org/

INDEX